Cooking for One

Cooking for One

Amy Willcock

EBURY
PRESS

1 3 5 7 9 10 8 6 4 2

Published in 2009 by Ebury Press,
an imprint of Ebury Publishing

A Random House Group Company

Text copyright © Amy Willcock 2009

Amy Willcock has asserted her right to be identified
as the author of this Work in accordance with the
Copyright, Designs and Patents Act 1988

The Random House Group Limited Reg. No. 954009

Addresses for companies within the Random House
Group can be found at
www.randomhouse.co.uk

A CIP catalogue record for this book is available from
the British Library

The Random House Group Limited supports The
Forest Stewardship Council (FSC), the leading
international forest certification organisation. All
our titles that are printed on Greenpeace-approved
FSC-certified paper carry the FSC logo. Our paper
procurement policy can be found at
www.rbooks.co.uk/environment

To buy books by your favourite authors and register for
offers visit www.rbooks.co.uk

Editor: Gillian Haslam
Designer: Isobel Gillan
Illustrator: Melvyn Evans

Printed and bound in Singapore by Tien Wah Press

ISBN 978-0-09-192671-7

AUTHOR'S ACKNOWLEDGEMENTS

My thanks go to Carey Smith, Judith Hannam,
Sarah Wooldridge, Gillian Haslam, Isobel Gillan
and, of course, my family.

contents

Introduction 6

treat yourself
Breakfast 10

less time
Snacks and Soup 15

more time
Snacks and Soup 26

less time
Meat and Poultry 34

more time
Meat and Poultry 59

less time
Fish and Seafood 86

more time
Fish and Seafood 106

less time
Vegetarian 122

more time
Vegetarian 146

treat yourself
Desserts and Baking 155

treat yourself
Drinks 166

Index 174

Introduction

TOO MANY PEOPLE just don't bother to cook for themselves when they are home alone, which is a real shame. The joy of cooking for one is that it takes less time, washing up is minimal, and occasionally you can splurge on luxuries such as lobster because you are only buying in small quantities.

This book is about treating yourself to good food and a fabulous table, even if you are eating alone. Creating a beautiful tray for supper in front of the telly or setting the table ready to tune in and have the radio as your guest can be hugely satisfying and enjoyable. The recipes and ideas here will be invaluable when all you need is food for one. Indeed, *Cooking for One* should be in every kitchen – it's just as appropriate if you are part of a big family but finding yourself on your own for a few days, or are a teenager, student or single person at home. Most of us find ourselves on our own at some time or another, so just think of cooking for one as a treat, as an opportunity to cook something you have always wanted to try or a chance to experiment with favourite ingredients.

When cooking my recipes, please don't feel you always have to follow them slavishly – treat them as inspiration and create your own variations. The main courses – meat, fish and vegetarian – are divided into chapters entitled 'More Time' and 'Less Time', so no matter how much time you have available, you will always find something to tempt you.

Location, Location, Location

Where you eat is really important and setting the table or a tray should be a pleasurable experience. When I'm at home on my own, I always make sure that I set the table or tray with a proper linen napkin and a flower – be it an arrangement, a single stem or simply a flowerhead floating in a glass.

It's also a good idea to vary the places where you eat. If you have a fireplace, set up a table nearby and enjoy dinner by the fire. Or if you have a garden or terrace, eat outside as much as possible. This may sounds obvious, but single friends I have spoken to often say they don't think this is worth bothering about. The setting, however, influences our enjoyment of food. Taking trouble over this will lift your spirits and make you feel special.

Shopping and the Single Cook

Shopping for the single cook is fantastic. Yes, you will have to buy the odd ingredient (such as puff pastry) that comes in a larger quantity than you will need, but you can freeze any leftovers or store them in the refrigerator. Vegetables and fruits can all be bought loose and I recommend buying seasonal, organic and locally grown food. Visit the local farmers' market or organic farm shop – many provide an organic box scheme suitable for one person if you ask.

Most of the single people I spoke to while researching this book liked to make the decision of what to eat for supper on the day and what they bought was influenced by the produce available or a recipe they had seen. Few planned each day's menu in advance. Of course, cooking extra portions is a great help when time is short as you can take something out of the freezer in the morning and cook it when you get home later on.

Keeping a well-stocked store cupboard is essential for the single cook. Having what you need to hand means you can pull together a healthy quick and delicious meal in no time at all. See the next page for a list of my store-cupboard essentials.

My favourite stand-by ingredients are:

Fridge

lemons

tomatoes

cucumber

bacon/pancetta

butter

double cream

Parmesan cheese

eggs

potatoes (baked pots in the freezer
too – see page 29 for instructions)

Freezer

bread – divide it up into 2 slices
wrapped in clingfilm so that you
only defrost what you need

individually wrapped chicken breasts,
chops and steaks

gravy – if you roast a chicken, make
gravy in the usual way and freeze
it in small batches

really good-quality sausages

peas and spinach

Store cupboard

risotto rice

dried pasta

ready-made gnocchi

easy-cook rice in 30g pouches

tinned tomatoes

dried porcini mushrooms

good-quality chicken and vegetable
stocks

tuna fish in olive oil

porridge

Plus fresh seasonal vegetables from an organic box scheme and pots of fresh
herbs on the kitchen windowsill.

A word about eggs

They are the most versatile food and a larder should not be without at least half a dozen eggs at all times! Buy good-quality free-range farm eggs from your local farmers' market or organic shop if possible.

Storage times for fresh food

Here are a few guidelines for how long foods will keep, assuming they start out in good condition and are well wrapped:
Cream: up to 5 days
Hard cheeses, well wrapped: 3–6 months
Butter: up to 7 weeks
Eggs: up to 1 month
Meat, poultry and fish: 3 days

If foods smell bad, has gone a strange colour or is growing mould, as the saying goes: if in doubt, throw it out!

Kitchen essentials

There are just a couple of pieces of kitchen equipment which I find really useful and are worth investing in:

* Invest in top-quality knives and always keep them sharp.
* A small electric non-stick frying pan is really useful if you have limited space.
* Stick blenders are great for soups and sauces and produce almost no washing up (always a plus point!).
* A good-quality wok can be used for many dishes, including stir-fries and curries.
* Invest in one really good copper saucepan. It will give you much pleasure every time you use it and produce delicious food.
* A mini food processor is also invaluable.

TREAT YOURSELF
Breakfast

Good Morning Muffins

This recipe makes 6 muffins – bake some for friends and freeze the rest in twos.

135g plain flour, sifted
1 tsp baking powder
35g golden caster sugar
pinch of salt
1 egg
50ml sunflower oil
85ml milk
80g blueberries
80g raspberries

Preheat the oven to 200°C/400°F/gas mark 6. Line a 6-hole muffin tin with muffin papers.

In a large bowl, thoroughly mix together all the ingredients. Spoon the mixture into the muffin tin, filling the papers to the top. Bake for 20–25 minutes or until they are golden. To test if they are cooked in the middle, insert the point of a knife or a skewer – if it comes out clean, they are ready. If the mixture is still loose, put them back in the oven for a few more minutes.

Remove from tin and cool on a wire rack.

To freeze, wrap in clingfilm or place in a small freezer bag when cool and freeze for up to 1 month.

Bircher Muesli

Muesli:
400g porridge oats
175g bran
180g toasted mixed nuts – such as almonds, walnuts, Brazil, etc
200g chopped mixed dried organic fruit – such as figs, apricots, apples, dates, etc

To serve:
1 small pot of natural yoghurt
Handful of fresh berries, such as strawberries, raspberries, blackberries
½ apple, grated
1 tsp toasted hazelnuts

Mix all the muesli ingredients together and store in an airtight tin.

To serve, mix a teacup of the muesli, natural yoghurt, berries, grated apple and hazelnuts together and stand overnight in the fridge or for an hour or so. Spoon into a glass bowl. Serve with more fresh fruit and honey.

Porridge

50g oatmeal
150ml milk

Put the oatmeal and milk into a saucepan with 150ml water and bring to the boil. Turn down the heat and simmer for about 5 minutes – it is important to cook the oatmeal.

Serve with double cream and brown sugar or yoghurt and honey. You can also add all sorts of other delicious goodies to the porridge, such as sultanas, desiccated coconut, toasted almonds, hazelnuts, dried cranberries – let your taste buds run wild!

Smoothies

For those mornings when food is too much of a chore to chew! A stick blender is one of my kitchen essentials as it is easy to use, takes up little space and is easy to clean! You will need a blender for smoothies made with crushed ice.

These are some of my favourite combinations – simply blend together:

- Seasonal fruits, milk or yoghurt and fruit juice.
- Apple juice, a grating of ginger and blueberries.
- Blueberries, pineapple juice, natural yoghurt and a touch of honey.

Refrigerator Bread

The great thing about this bread is that you can pull off small amounts to bake and leave the rest in the fridge for up to 3 days. You can also freeze any leftover dough and use it for pizza bases or quick flat breads.

1kg strong bread flour
30g butter, softened
30ml sunflower oil, plus extra for greasing
25g salt
35g fresh yeast

Put the dough hook into an electric mixer and add the flour, butter, oil and salt to the mixer bowl. Mix to combine. Crumble the yeast into 425ml warm water, stir and when the yeast has melted, pour it into the flour. Add up to 175ml additional warm water if the dough is too stiff. It is always best to hold back a little water and add it if necessary, rather than pour it all in and have to add more flour. Knead for 8 minutes on a medium speed or until the dough is soft and elastic. Lightly oil a bowl and pop the dough inside it. Cover with clingfilm and store in the fridge overnight.

When you are ready to bake the bread, remove however much you want of the dough from the fridge and mould into shape on a piece of Bake-O-Glide or in a tin. Let it rise in a warm place for about 45–60 minutes or until it has doubled in size.

Preheat the oven to 200°C/400°F/gas mark 6.

Bake the bread for 20 minutes or until it sounds hollow when tapped on the underside. Cool on a wire rack.

LESS TIME
Snacks and Soup

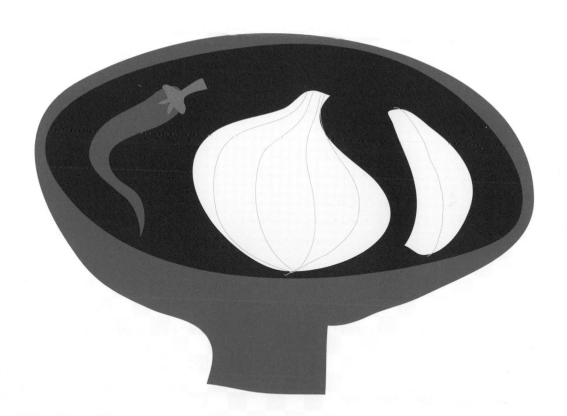

Sweet, Hot and Sour Melon with Prosciutto

1 tbsp mint jelly
The tip of a bird's eye chilli, finely chopped
Tiny piece of garlic, chopped
½ cantaloupe melon, very ripe
3 slices of prosciutto
2 fresh mint leaves, finely chopped
Focaccia bread, to serve

Heat up the mint jelly, chilli and garlic with 1 tablespoon of water in a pan and simmer for 1 minute. Set aside to cool completely.

Cut the melon into long slices and remove the skin. Arrange the melon on a plate and drape the prosciutto over it. Spoon over the cooled sauce and garnish with the chopped mint. Serve with focaccia bread.

French Toast
with Fried Tomatoes

1 beefsteak tomato, halved
1 Portobello mushroom
A little oil
1 egg
2 tbsp milk
Salt and freshly ground black pepper
1 thick slice of delicious white bread
A little butter
25g Cheddar cheese, grated

Preheat the grill to its highest setting.

Fry the tomato and the mushroom in a little oil, then set aside and keep warm.

Beat the egg with the milk in a shallow dish and season with salt and pepper. Dip the bread in the egg mix and soak it well. Fry the bread in the frying pan with a little butter until it is golden – about 1½ minutes on each side. Top the French toast with the tomato and scatter with the cheese, then grill for a few minutes until it has melted. Serve with the fried Portobello mushroom.

Croque Monsieur

2 slices of sourdough bread
Clarified butter
50g Gruyère cheese, grated
3–4 thin slices of really good ham

The trick with this is to make sure the slices of bread are the same size and fit together perfectly.

Heat a cast-iron or heavy-based frying pan over a medium heat.

Spread the bread thinly on both sides with the clarified butter. Scatter half the cheese over one slice of bread, then add the ham slices followed by the rest of the cheese. Cover with the other slice of bread and press down firmly. Place in the hot pan and turn down the heat if it is too high. Cover with a large lid. Cook for 1–2 minutes until golden brown, then flip over and continue cooking until the cheese has melted. Eat immediately while still hot.

Variations

To make a Croque Madame, top the finished sandwich with a fried egg.

Sometimes I make a thick white sauce and add the cheese to it, let it cool and then continue to make the sandwich, spreading the sauce over one slice of bread, then topping with the ham and remaining slice of bread.

Alpine Eggs

Softened butter, for greasing
Salt and freshly ground black pepper
1 large egg
1 tbsp double cream
30g Gruyère cheese, grated
A few snipped fresh chives, optional

Preheat the oven to 190°C/375°F/gas mark 5.

Generously butter a shallow ovenproof dish with the butter. Sprinkle the salt and pepper on to the bottom of the dish. Break the egg into the dish, then spoon over the cream and scatter over the cheese.

Place the dish on a shallow baking tray and bake for 4–5 minutes or until the egg has set. If you wish, sprinkle with snipped chives before serving.

Potted Kippers on Toast

1 flaked kipper, all bones removed
15g unsalted butter, softened
Freshly ground black pepper
1½ tbsp cream cheese
1½ tsp double cream
1 tsp anchovy sauce
Pinch of caster sugar
Squeeze of lemon juice, to taste
Hot buttered toast, to serve

Put the kipper, butter, pepper, cream cheese, cream, anchovy sauce, sugar and lemon juice into a bowl and mash with a fork until smooth, or you can use a pestle and mortar. Check the consistency – you want a smooth pâté, not too loose nor too stiff; if it is too stiff add some more double cream. Check the seasoning. Pour it into a dish and serve with hot buttered toast.

Devils on Horseback

4 rashers of rindless streaky bacon
1 tbsp mango chutney
4 tbsp cream cheese
8 stoned ready-to-eat organic prunes

Preheat the oven to 220°C/425°F/gas mark 7. Line a small, shallow baking tray with Bake-O-Glide. Lay the bacon rashers on a flat surface and stretch them out by running the back of a knife along their length, then cut each piece in half. Put a little of the chutney and cream cheese into each prune, then wrap the prunes in the bacon and lay them on the baking tray. Cook for 10–12 minutes or until they are browned. Serve on a bed of rice with a green salad.

Grilled Figs wrapped in Parma Ham with Gorgonzola

2–3 fresh plump ripe figs
50g Gorgonzola cheese, cut into chunks
1–2 fresh thyme sprigs
2–3 slices of Parma ham
Balsamic vinegar
Olive oil
Freshly ground black pepper
1–2 slices focaccia bread, toasted
1 clove of garlic, peeled and cut in half

Cut the figs into quarters but leave the bases intact so that they hold together. Place a slice of Gorgonzola on top of each one and push in a few thyme leaves, then wrap up the fig in the Parma ham. Drizzle over a little balsamic vinegar and olive oil and season with black pepper.

Toast the bread and rub with the cut edge of the garlic. Place a fig parcel on the toast. Preheat the grill to its highest setting and grill the figs for 1 minute. Great served with a rocket salad.

Tomato and Bread Soup

For this to be truly delicious, you must use the best tomatoes so choose them carefully – they should smell like tomatoes and feel heavy. The soup's original name is pappa al pomodoro.

1–1½ cloves of garlic, peeled and sliced
1 tbsp good-quality olive oil, plus extra to serve
3 very ripe tomatoes, skinned and seeded
Salt and freshly ground black pepper
1–2 slices of stale sourdough or ciabatta bread, crusts removed
   and roughly torn into pieces
6 basil leaves
Freshly grated Parmesan cheese, to serve

Put the garlic and the olive oil into a large saucepan and cook very gently for 2–3 minutes. Do not let the garlic burn or go brown. Add the tomatoes. Stir and simmer for about 5 minutes. The tomatoes will become very concentrated. Season with salt and pepper, then add 100ml water and bring up to the boil. Check the seasoning. Add the bread and stir to combine well. Add more water if it is too thick.

Remove from the heat and tear in the basil leaves. Stir again. Add a good glug of olive oil and stir. Ladle into a bowl and sprinkle with Parmesan cheese.

To skin a tomato, put it into a bowl and pour boiling water over. Leave for a few minutes, then remove from the water. Wearing rubber gloves, carefully peel off the skin. Cut in half and scoop out the seeds.

Things on Toast

Really good bread toasted, a piece of cheese and some great home-made chutney is all you need to have a feast, but here are a few other ideas. These combinations also work well as open sandwiches.

- Grilled radicchio, Gorgonzola cheese and walnuts drizzled with honey on toasted walnut bread.
- Pan-fried mushrooms, parsley and Taleggio cheese on toasted ciabatta.
- Sautéed chicken livers with bacon and celery on toasted sourdough.
- Braised leeks with hard-boiled eggs and anchovies on toasted sourdough.
- Grilled peppers and pesto with melted mozzarella cheese on toasted focaccia.
- Roasted beetroot with grilled goats' cheese, walnuts and honey on toasted walnut and raisin bread.
- Scrambled eggs with pancetta and grilled mushrooms on a toasted muffin.

Potted Ham and Cheese with Sourdough Toast

150g ham, carved off the bone, all fat removed
50g mature Cheddar cheese, grated
1½ tsp white wine
25g butter
Pinch of cayenne pepper
½ tbsp chopped fresh flat-leaf parsley
Sourdough toast, to serve

Put all the ingredients into the bowl of a mini food processor and whiz until smooth, or you can use a pestle and mortar. Check the consistency – you want a smooth pâté, neither too loose nor too stiff. Check the seasoning. Spoon into a ramekin and serve with sourdough toast.

If you wish, pour over a little clarified butter to seal the top and refrigerate for 2–3 days.

Worcestershire Toast

55g mature Cheddar cheese, grated
1 apple, grated
½ tbsp Worcestershire sauce
½ tbsp double cream
Salt and freshly ground black pepper
2 rashers of cooked bacon
1–2 thick slices of buttered toast

Preheat the grill to its highest setting.

Mix the cheese, apple, Worcestershire sauce and cream in a bowl, and season with salt and pepper. Place the cooked bacon onto the buttered toast and spoon over the cheese mixture. Heat under the grill until the sauce is bubbling and golden.

MORE TIME
Snacks and Soup

Artichoke Hearts on Toast

1 clove of garlic, peeled
1 anchovy fillet
1 egg
Juice of 1 lemon
175ml olive oil
2–3 artichoke hearts in olive oil
1 tbsp mayonnaise (see page 78)
60g Parmesan cheese, grated
2 slices of sourdough bread, toasted

To make the marinade, put the garlic, anchovy, its oil, the egg and lemon juice into a mini food processor or use a stick blender and blitz. Pour in the olive oil in a steady stream.

Cut the artichoke hearts in half, place in a non-metallic bowl and pour over the marinade. Leave them to marinate in a cool place overnight.

When you are ready to cook, preheat the grill to its highest setting. Mix the mayonnaise and Parmesan together in a bowl. Spread the toasted bread with half the mayonnaise and place the artichokes on top, then spoon the remaining mayonnaise on top. Place the toasts on a shallow baking tray and slide the tray on to a high runner. Grill for 2–3 minutes or until they start to go brown on top. Serve warm.

Freeze artisan breads in small quantities or slices for fast defrosting.

Bacon, Lettuce, Avocado and Tomato Sandwich with Fried Onion Rings

2 slices of good white bread, toasted
Mayonnaise (see page 78)
2–3 rashers of cooked smoked bacon
A few leaves of crisp iceberg lettuce
½ a ripe avocado, sliced
2–3 slices of beefsteak tomato

Fried onion rings:
2 egg whites
140g plain flour, sifted
Pinch of salt
Ice-cold lager
Sunflower oil
1 large onion, peeled, cut into thick slices and separated

Make the sandwich first, then fry the onion rings.

Spread the toast with mayonnaise, then layer one slice with the bacon, lettuce, avocado and tomato. Top with the second piece of toast and cut into four.

Whisk the egg whites in a bowl with a fork until frothy, then add the flour, salt and enough ice-cold lager to bring the mixture up to 250ml. Mix together lightly with the fork to make a lumpy batter.

Pour the oil into a deep pan to a depth of 4cm and heat. Test the temperature of the oil by dripping in a little batter – if it crisps up immediately, the oil is hot enough.

Dip an onion slice into the batter and quickly lower it into the hot oil. Count to about 10 and it should be golden. Lift out on to a piece of kitchen paper, and repeat until all the onion slices are cooked. You can fry 2–3 onion slices at a time, but don't overcrowd the pan as this would lower the temperature of the oil too much and the batter would go flabby instead of being light and crisp.

Sprinkle with salt and serve with the sandwich.

Frozen Baked Potatoes

These are really versatile and are the ultimate get-ahead supper – just remove one from the freezer before going out to work and cook when you get home. I make these in batches. See overleaf for more ideas for toppings.

Baking potatoes
Butter
Salt and freshly ground black pepper
Grated Cheddar cheese

Preheat the oven to 200°C/400°F/gas mark 6.

Scrub the potatoes and bake for about 45 minutes, until soft. Remove from the oven and cut them in half lengthways. When they are cool enough to handle, scoop out the potato into a bowl, taking care not to break the skins, and mash until smooth. Beat in butter, salt, pepper and grated Cheddar cheese. Fill the skins with the potato mix, place on a tray and open-freeze them. When they're frozen, bag them up and store in the freezer.

When you are ready to cook the potatoes, thaw them for 1 hour, then bake in a moderate oven for 20–25 minutes or until piping hot.

Toppings for Baked Potatoes

Fried mushrooms and bacon

½ tbsp sunflower oil
1 rasher of bacon, chopped
2–3 mushrooms, cut in half
Knob of butter
Dash of cream, optional
Salt and freshly ground black pepper

Heat the oil in a frying pan and fry the bacon and mushrooms for 3–5 minutes. Add the butter and a little cream, season with salt and pepper and serve over a baked potato with some butter mashed into it.

Welsh rarebit topping

Top an open baked potato with Welsh rarebit topping (see page 61) and place the potato under a hot grill until it is bubbling.

Tomato and basil topping

1 tbsp olive oil
6 cherry tomatoes
2–3 fresh basil leaves
1 tsp prepared garlic
Salt and freshly ground black pepper
1 slice of mozzarella cheese

Heat the oil in a frying pan and toss in the tomatoes, basil and garlic. Cook for 5 minutes or until the tomatoes start to burst. Do not let the garlic burn. Season with salt and pepper and spoon into an open baked potato. Top with the mozzarella cheese and grill for a few minutes until the cheese starts to melt.

Classic sour cream and chives

2 tbsp sour cream
½ tbsp snipped fresh chives
Salt and freshly ground black pepper

Mix the sour cream, chives, salt and pepper together and spoon into an open baked potato that has already had butter mashed into it. You can also chop up a little smoked salmon or caviar and mix it with the sour cream.

Sun-dried tomato and black olive topping

Leaves from a sprig of fresh thyme
3 sun-dried tomatoes, chopped
6–8 black olives, stoned and chopped
2–3 anchovies, chopped
Freshly ground black pepper
1 tsp prepared garlic
1 tbsp grated Parmesan cheese

Put everything except the Parmesan into a mini food processor and blitz. Spoon over an open baked potato and sprinkle over the cheese.

Store potatoes in a cool dark place and not in plastic bags or in the fridge.

Chilled Tomato Soup with Cucumber and Crab

10cm piece of cucumber, peeled, seeded and diced
Salt
1 tbsp single cream
1 tbsp natural yoghurt
100ml tomato juice, chilled
100ml chicken stock, chilled (make with a good-quality chicken cube)
Dash of Tabasco sauce
75g white crabmeat plus 1 claw (or 2 if you are feeling greedy!)
½ tbsp chopped fresh dill
Water biscuits, to serve

Chilled soup should be served in a cold bowl, so place a serving bowl in the fridge before you start making it.

Degorge the cucumber dice by placing them in a colander set over a bowl and sprinkling with salt. Leave to drain for about 15 minutes – this will draw out any excess moisture.

Whisk the cream and yoghurt together until smooth, then stir in the tomato juice, chicken stock, and season with the Tabasco. Add the drained cucumber and leave to infuse for about 15 minutes.

Remove the chilled bowl from the fridge and spoon in the crabmeat and the claw. Stir the soup if it has settled, taste for seasoning and adjust. Ladle the soup over the crabmeat and garnish with the chopped dill. Serve with water biscuits.

Fennel and Lentil Soup

45g brown lentils
45g green lentils
1 clove of garlic, unpeeled
1 carrot, peeled and diced
1 small fennel bulb, peeled and quartered
¼ tsp sweet paprika
500ml chicken stock
Salt and freshly ground black pepper
1 tbsp olive oil
1 tbsp roughly chopped fresh flat-leaf parsley
Sourdough bread, to serve

Wash the lentils and pick through them, removing any little stones. Put the lentils, garlic clove still in its papery skin, carrot, fennel, paprika, stock and a good grinding of pepper into a saucepan. Bring to the boil, then turn down to a simmer for 25 minutes. Check occasionally and add a little boiling water if it needs it.

Scoop out the garlic and squeeze the pulp from the skin back into the lentil soup. Taste for seasoning and add salt if necessary. Add the olive oil and stir in the parsley. Ladle into a bowl and drizzle over more olive oil. Serve with sourdough bread.

LESS TIME
Meat and Poultry

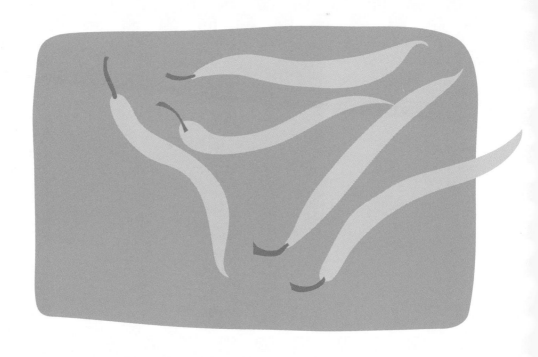

Spring Pork Stir-fry

2 tsp sunflower oil
1 tsp sesame oil
1 pork loin steak, cut into strips
3 spears of asparagus, trimmed and cut into 4cm pieces
1 spring onion, trimmed and finely chopped
50g sugar snap peas, finely sliced
3cm piece of fresh ginger, peeled
1 small clove of garlic, peeled
½ tbsp honey
A splash of soy sauce
1 head of bok choy, roughly shredded
5–6 fresh mint leaves, shredded
½ tsp sesame seeds
Jasmine rice, to serve

Heat a high-sided frying pan or wok until searingly hot. Add the oils and quickly fry the pork, moving the pieces around the pan, until cooked through. Transfer to a warm plate, cover with clingfilm and set aside to keep warm.

Next add the asparagus, spring onion and sugar snap peas, quickly moving them around the pan. Grate in the ginger and garlic. Add the honey and soy sauce, then the bok choy. Stir in the pork, then remove from the heat and add the mint and sesame seeds. Serve immediately with a bowl of jasmine rice.

I recommend investing in a really good non-stick wok. You can use it for stir-fries as well as curries, and even moules marinière.

Steak or Chops with Savoury Butter

1 rib eye steak or fillet, or 1 pork or lamb chop
Salt and freshly ground black pepper

Herb butter:
250g unsalted butter, softened
Sea salt and freshly ground black pepper
3 tbsp chopped mixed fresh herbs, such as parsley, rosemary, thyme and
    marjoram, or just one herb, such as tarragon
A squeeze of lemon juice
1 clove of garlic, peeled and crushed, optional

Spiced butter:
250g unsalted butter, softened
1 tbsp Worcestershire sauce
Sea salt and freshly ground black pepper
2 tbsp chopped fresh parsley
A squeeze of lemon juice
2–6 dashes of Tabasco sauce, to taste

To make the herb or spiced butter, mix everything well with a fork. Mould into a log shape, wrap with clingfilm and freeze for up to 3 months. When you want to use it, slice a piece off and use as required.

To cook the steak, heat the grill pan until it is smoking. Season the steak with salt and pepper and cook the steak to your liking. A medium steak will take about 2 minutes on each side, but cook it for a longer or shorter time according to your taste. Always rest the steak for at least 2 minutes in a warm dish before serving so that the meat relaxes and isn't tough.

Pork chops are best cooked in a grill pan, too. Use the same method as for steak but cook the chops for about 3 minutes on each side. Rest for at least 2 minutes before serving.

For lamb chops, you may only need to cook for 1–2 minutes on each side, according to how pink you like your meat.

Serve the griddled meat with savoury butters.

Autumn Apples and Bacon

A splash of sunflower oil
3 rashers of back bacon
1 eating apple, peeled, cored and sliced
2–3 thick slices of Cheddar cheese

Preheat the grill.

Heat the oil in an ovenproof frying pan over a medium heat and fry the bacon until crispy. Remove the bacon, add the apple slices to the pan and cook for 3 minutes, turning halfway through cooking. Drain any excess fat from the pan, then place the bacon on top of the apple slices and top with the cheese. Grill until the cheese just begins to melt. Serve with a salad of curly endive dressed with a splash of balsamic vinegar.

Blue Cheese Burger

100g good-quality beef, such as rump steak
A dash of Worcestershire sauce
Salt and freshly ground black pepper
25g blue cheese (Danish blue is a good choice as it holds together well)
1 soft white bap
A little olive oil
1½ tsp spicy tomato chutney
Slice of tomato
Iceberg lettuce leaf

Put the beef into a food processor and pulse so that it is minced, but do not overwork it. Transfer to a bowl and add a dash of Worcestershire sauce and some salt and pepper. Mix it well with your hands, then form it around the cube of blue cheese to make a patty shape. Place in the fridge for at least 10 minutes, or longer if you have time.

Heat up a grill pan so that it is smoking. Split the bap in half, toast the inside and set aside. Take the burger out of the fridge. Put a little olive oil on your hands and gently massage into the burger. Cook on the grill pan for about 2–3 minutes on each side.

Spread the chutney on the lower half of the bap, then add the tomato slice, the burger, then the lettuce. Top with the other half of the bap.

Veal Saltimbocca

2 thin slices of prosciutto
175g slice of veal, beaten out a little
1 sage leaf
Salt and freshly ground black pepper
1 tbsp olive oil
A knob of butter
Radicchio, to serve
Balsamic vinegar, to serve

Lay the prosciutto slices on top of the veal, then add the sage leaf. Secure them with a toothpick. Season with salt and pepper

Heat the oil and butter in a frying pan until frothy. Fry the veal for about 2 minutes on each side. Serve with a salad of radicchio dressed in balsamic vinegar, good olive oil and any pan juices.

Always buy the best you can afford - good-quality ingredients need very little done to them to be superb!

Escalope of Veal with Tarragon Sauce

175g escalope of veal, beaten out
1 tbsp plain flour
1 tbsp sunflower oil
A knob of butter
Splash of white wine (about ¼ of a glass)
Salt and freshly ground black pepper
1 clove of garlic, peeled
70ml double cream
3 stalks of fresh tarragon, plus 1 tsp chopped tarragon

Dust the veal with the flour, shaking off any excess.

Heat a frying pan so that it is very hot, then add the sunflower oil and butter and fry the veal – about 1½ minutes per side. Set aside and keep warm.

Drain off any excess fat from the pan, then add the white wine. Season with salt and pepper and add the whole garlic clove, cream and the tarragon stalks. Bring up to the boil, then turn down and simmer for 3 minutes or until the sauce has reduced by half. When it is ready, transfer the veal to a warm plate, pouring any plate juices into the sauce. Pour over the sauce and sprinkle over the chopped tarragon. Serve with new potatoes and peas.

Calves' Liver and Bacon

Calves' liver is a great freezer stand-by because you can freeze it in slices and it defrosts in about 10 minutes.

½ tbsp plain flour
Salt
Sunflower oil
2 rashers of back bacon
25g butter
1 small onion or shallot, peeled and thinly sliced
Tomato ketchup
200g calves' liver, sliced, all the tubes, membranes and veins removed
   (you can ask the butcher to do this for you)

Spoon the flour on to a plate and season with salt. Pour about a tablespoon of oil into a heavy-based frying pan and heat it up over a medium heat. When it is very hot, add the bacon and fry until it is crispy around the edges. Remove the bacon and set aside on a warmed plate.

Add a knob of the butter to the fat and when it foams, add the onion or shallot and fry until soft and slightly charred around the edges. Add a squeeze of ketchup and stir well. Spoon on to the plate with the bacon.

Dust the liver slices with the seasoned flour. Wipe out the pan with kitchen paper, pour in another tablespoon of oil and add the remaining butter to the pan. Heat this until frothy, add the liver and fry for a few minutes on each side, depending how thick the slices are. The liver should still be pink inside – if you overcook it, it will become tough. Transfer the liver to a warm plate and top with the onions and bacon. Great served with mashed potato.

Loin of Lamb with Parmesan and Basil Crust

1 shallot, peeled
1 rasher of smoked bacon
½ clove of garlic, peeled
3–4 fresh basil leaves
3–4 fresh mint leaves
1 tbsp butter
Salt and freshly ground black pepper
1½ tbsp freshly grated Parmesan cheese
2 tbsp fresh breadcrumbs
175g piece of lamb fillet (not neck fillet)

Preheat the oven to 200°C/400°F/gas mark 6.

Put the shallot, bacon, garlic, herbs, butter, salt and pepper into the bowl of a food processor. Whiz until everything is thoroughly chopped and combined. Remove the blade and mix in the Parmesan and the breadcrumbs. Press the mixture onto the lamb fillet.

Place the lamb on a baking tray and cook for 12–15 minutes or until cooked to your liking. Serve with new potatoes, courgettes and broad beans. This recipe also works well with pork fillet.

Always have a bag of breadcrumbs in the freezer to use for quick crunchy toppings.

Pan-fried Chicken Livers with Tomatoes

A knob of butter
1 tbsp sunflower oil or some oil from the sun-dried tomato jar
1 small onion or large shallot, peeled and thinly sliced
1 tbsp pancetta cubes
5 chicken livers
5–6 cherry tomatoes, cut in half
2–3 sun-dried tomatoes, roughly chopped
Freshly ground black pepper
A little chopped fresh flat-leaf parsley
Sourdough toast, to serve

Melt the butter in a frying pan with some oil over a medium-high heat and fry the onion until soft and just starting to colour. Add the pancetta cubes and cook until they are just beginning to colour, then add the chicken livers and tomatoes and cook for 1–2 minutes – the chicken livers should still be pink. Don't overcook them whatever you do! Season with black pepper and sprinkle with parsley. Serve on a warm plate with hot sourdough toast.

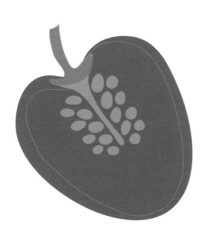

Chicken with Creamy Mustard Sauce

1 tbsp sunflower oil
1 chicken leg, including thigh, skin left on

Mustard sauce:
25g butter
25g plain flour
50ml hot chicken stock
1 heaped tsp Dijon mustard
75ml double cream

Preheat the oven to 180°C/350°F/gas mark 4.

To make the sauce, melt the butter in a small saucepan. Add the flour and stir briskly to make a roux. Add the hot stock a little at a time, whisking constantly. The sauce should be thick and glossy. Simmer for 2–3 minutes. Stir in the mustard and cream and simmer for 1 minute, then set aside.

Heat the sunflower oil in a frying pan, add the chicken and brown on all sides, then transfer to an ovenproof dish and pour over the mustard sauce. Cook the chicken in the oven for 20 minutes or until the sauce is bubbling and starting to brown on top and the chicken is cooked through. Serve with basmati rice.

Chicken and Roquefort Salad

2 heads of little gem lettuce
2 slices of stale ciabatta bread
50g Roquefort cheese, cut into cubes
6 walnut halves, chopped
1 cooked chicken leg
Salt and freshly ground black pepper

Vinaigrette:
1 tbsp red wine vinegar
2 tbsp sunflower oil
1 tbsp olive oil
½ tsp sugar
½ tsp salt
1 tsp Dijon mustard

Whisk all the vinaigrette ingredients together in a bowl or shake in a jar.
(Any unused vinaigrette will keep in the fridge for at least a month.)

Tear up the lettuce and the bread and put in a bowl. Add the cheese and
walnuts. Tear the meat from the chicken leg and add to the bowl. Toss in
2 tablespoons of the vinaigrette. Taste and season. Transfer to a plate and
eat in the garden!

Chicken Milanese with Fennel Slaw

1 chicken breast
2 slices of day-old bread from a country-style loaf,
   whizzed in a blender and made into breadcrumbs
1 tbsp grated Parmesan cheese
1 tsp lemon zest
½ tsp chopped parsley
Good grating of fresh garlic (about ½ clove)
1 tbsp plain flour
Salt and freshly ground black pepper
1 tbsp Dijon mustard
1 egg, beaten
2–3 tbsp sunflower oil
A knob of butter

Fennel slaw:
1 lemon
1 baby bulb of fennel
Extra virgin olive oil

To make the fennel slaw, slice the baby fennel very thinly and drizzle over a little olive oil and a good squeeze of lemon juice, then season with salt and pepper.

Using a sharp knife, carefully slice the chicken breast horizontally nearly all the way through, then open out like a book. Place it between two pieces of clingfilm and beat it out flat with a rolling pin.

Mix the breadcrumbs with the Parmesan, lemon zest, parsley and garlic, then spread onto a clean piece of clingfilm. Tip the flour on to a clean piece of clingfilm and season with salt and pepper.

Spread both sides of the chicken fillet with the mustard, then dip into the flour. Shake off any excess, then dip into the egg and finally into the breadcrumbs. (If you wish, you can do this in advance and store in the fridge.)

Heat the sunflower oil and butter in a frying pan and cook the chicken for about 2–3 minutes on each side so that it is cooked through and crispy. Drain on kitchen paper and serve with the fennel slaw and a wedge of lemon.

Chicken and Broccoli Bake

Butter, for greasing
50g broccoli, or purple sprouting broccoli or asparagus in season
100g cooked chicken, skinned and cut into pieces
1 tbsp crème fraîche
1 tbsp mayonnaise
Salt and freshly ground black pepper
1 tbsp grated Parmesan cheese
1 tbsp grated strong Cheddar cheese
Sprinkling of breadcrumbs, optional

Preheat the oven to 190°C/375°F/gas mark 5. Butter an ovenproof dish.

Cook the broccoli in a pan of boiling water until it still has a bit of a bite. Drain and set aside.

Put the chicken into the dish and lay the broccoli on top. Mix together the crème fraîche and mayonnaise and season with salt and pepper. Spoon this over the chicken and then top with the Cheddar, Parmesan and breadcrumbs, if using. Bake in the oven for 20 minutes or until it is hot and golden.

Order a weekly organic vegetable box to get the best seasonal produce.

Chicken and Apricot Salad with Lemon and Poppy Seed Dressing

175g cooked chicken breast, skinned and cut into chunks
1 tsp snipped fresh chives
2–3 fresh apricots, stoned and cut or torn into slices
Rocket, to serve

Dressing:
Juice and zest of 1 lemon
Salt and freshly ground black pepper
1 tsp poppy seeds
2 tbsp sour cream
1 tbsp olive oil
2 tbsp sunflower oil
1 tsp honey

To make the dressing, mix all the ingredients together. This will make more than you need, but store the remainder in the fridge for another day.

Put the chicken into a bowl and fold in 2 tablespoons of the dressing, the chives and apricots. Serve on a plate of rocket.

Chicken Salad
with Honey and Almond Dressing

1 tbsp sunflower oil
1 rasher of smoked bacon, chopped
1 chicken breast, skinned and sliced
Handful of mixed leaf salad or rocket
1 tbsp almonds, toasted in a dry frying pan

Dressing:
1 tbsp honey
1 tbsp white wine vinegar
1 tbsp walnut oil
2 tbsp sunflower oil
Salt and freshly ground black pepper

First, make the dressing. Whisk together the honey, white wine vinegar and the oils, season with salt and pepper and set aside.

Heat the sunflower oil in a frying pan until smoking hot. Quickly fry the bacon until crispy, then remove with a slotted spoon and set aside. Add the chicken slices to the pan. When they are cooked through, pour in 2 tablespoons of the honey dressing, add the cooked bacon and bring up to a gentle bubble. (Any remaining dressing can be kept in the fridge for a couple of days.)

Arrange the salad leaves on a plate and spoon over the warm chicken and bacon. Sprinkle with the toasted almonds and serve.

Devilled Chicken or Pheasant

This is a great recipe for leftover cooked chicken or pheasant.

175g cooked chicken or pheasant, torn into pieces, bones removed
1 tbsp Worcestershire sauce
1 tbsp mango chutney
¼ tsp English mustard
1 tsp mild curry paste or powder
100ml double cream
Salt and freshly ground black pepper
1 tsp chopped fresh parsley

Preheat the oven to 190°C/375°F/gas mark 5.

Arrange the meat in a deep ovenproof dish. Mix the Worcestershire sauce, chutney, mustard and curry paste together.

Whip the cream into soft peaks, then add the mango chutney mix and fold in well. Season with salt and pepper. Pour the sauce over the chicken and bake for 15 minutes or until the sauce is bubbling and starts to brown on top. Garnish with the parsley and serve with rice.

For delicacies such as partridge or pheasant, buy directly from a local shoot.

Chicken with Honey and Orange

1 chicken breast, skin on
1 tsp runny honey
A little oil and butter
Zest of ½ orange
Juice of 1 orange
1½ tbsp dry cider
Dash of soy sauce
Pinch of allspice
75ml chicken stock
Freshly ground black pepper

Preheat the oven to 190°C/375°F/gas mark 5.

Brush the chicken breast with the honey. Heat up a little oil and butter in an oven-proof frying pan and brown the chicken breast. Remove from the heat and pour off any excess fat. Add the orange zest and juice, cider, soy sauce, allspice and chicken stock to the pan, return to the heat and bring up to the boil; season with pepper. Put the pan in the oven and cook for about 8–10 minutes. Serve with boiled wild rice and an orange slice to garnish.

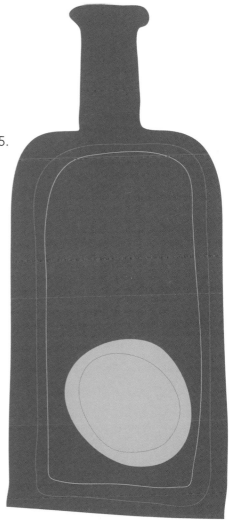

Chicken with Apricots and Prunes

Olive oil, for frying
1 rasher of smoked bacon, chopped, or pancetta
1 chicken leg, including thigh
1 shallot, peeled and sliced
2 no-soak prunes, cut in half
2 no-soak apricots, cut in half
¼ tsp chopped fresh rosemary
100ml chicken stock
Splash of white wine
Salt and freshly ground black pepper

Heat up a little oil in a frying pan with a lid and fry the bacon. Remove with a slotted spoon and set aside. Add the chicken leg to the pan and brown on all sides. Remove from the pan and set aside with the bacon. Fry the shallot until soft and staring to go brown around the edges. Drain off any excess fat.

Put the chicken and bacon back into the pan and add the prunes, apricots, rosemary, stock and white wine. Season with salt and pepper. Bring everything up to a boil and cover. Cook for 15 minutes or until the chicken leg is cooked through. Serve with boiled rice.

Pheasant with Chestnuts and Thyme

1 tbsp clarified butter or sunflower oil
1 rasher of smoked bacon, chopped
1 shallot, peeled and chopped
1 pheasant breast
75ml cider
75ml game or chicken stock
15–20g vacuum-packed chestnuts
1 sprig of fresh thyme
Salt and freshly ground black pepper
1 tbsp double cream

Heat the clarified butter or oil in a frying pan, add the bacon and shallot and cook until lightly browned. Remove them with a slotted spoon and set aside. Add the pheasant to the pan and cook for 2–3 minutes on each side or until it is cooked and no blood runs out. Remove and allow to rest while you make the sauce.

Add the cider to the pan and bubble for 1 minute, then add the shallot and bacon, stock, chestnuts, thyme, salt and pepper. Bring up to a simmer and bubble for 1–2 minutes. Taste and adjust the seasoning. Remove from the heat and stir in the cream.

Slice the pheasant breast and arrange on a plate, then spoon over the sauce. Great served with mashed potato.

Pan-fried Pigeon Breast
with Blackberries and Cassis

Splash of sunflower oil
1 shallot, peeled and chopped
2–3 pigeon breasts (available from butchers or some supermarkets)
Salt and freshly ground black pepper
A knob of butter
50ml chicken stock
1½ tbsp cassis
Handful of blackberries

Heat the oil in a frying pan and fry the shallot until it is just starting to
caramelise around the edges. Remove with a slotted spoon and set aside.
Season the pigeon breasts with some salt and increase the heat under the
pan. Put the pigeon breasts into the pan with the butter and fry to your liking –
usually 1–2 minutes on each side. Move to a warm plate, cover with clingfilm
and leave to rest.

Drain off any excess fat from the pan, leaving behind any crusty bits, and deglaze
the pan with the chicken stock and cassis. Return the shallot to the pan and
bubble to reduce for 3 minutes. Add the pigeon breasts and blackberries and
toss gently together. Serve with mashed potato and peas.

*If you need to prepare a partridge, pigeon
or pheasant, it is easier if you wet your hands
before plucking.*

Bubble and Squeak

Traditionally this was made with leftover potatoes and cabbage, but other leftover veg can be used too.

1 large potato, peeled and cut into chunks
¼ head of a small cabbage, sliced into medium pieces
Salt and freshly ground black pepper
Small knob of butter
1 tbsp sunflower oil
2 rashers of bacon
25g Cheddar cheese, grated

Put the potato into a saucepan of water and bring to the boil, then cook until it is soft but not falling apart. When it is 3–4 minutes from being ready, add the cabbage and cook until both cabbage and potato are done. Drain well. Tip them into a bowl, mash together roughly and season with salt and pepper.

Melt the butter and sunflower oil together in a frying pan and cook the bacon. Remove from the pan, drain on kitchen paper and keep warm. Use the same pan to cook the bubble and squeak. Using your hands, form the potato mix into a patty and fry it in the bacon fat for about 3 minutes on each side – it should be golden and brown.

Transfer the bubble and squeak to a warm plate and top with the bacon rashers. Scatter over the Cheddar cheese and enjoy.

Broad Beans with Prosciutto and Ricotta Cheese

1kg broad beans
Salt and freshly ground black pepper
100g fresh ricotta cheese
Aged balsamic vinegar
Good-quality olive oil
3–4 slices prosciutto
½ tbsp toasted pine nuts
Crusty bread, to serve

First, shell and pod the broad beans. Have a bowl of iced water ready for blanching. Shell the beans from the tough pod. Bring a pan of water up to the boil and cook the beans in salted boiling water for 2–3 minutes or until they start to wrinkle but still have a bit of bite to them. Remove the beans with a slotted spoon and plunge them into the iced water immediately. After a minute or so, drain from the iced water, carefully peel off the membrane and put the bright green beans into a bowl. This can be done in advance if you wish.

Crumble the ricotta cheese over the podded beans. Drizzle over some balsamic vinegar and olive oil and season with salt and pepper.

Arrange the prosciutto on a plate, spoon over the beans and cheese and scatter over the pine nuts. Serve with lots of crusty bread.

Mac and Cheese

50g macaroni
Salt
125ml thick double cream
50g Parmesan cheese, grated, plus a little extra for the topping
50g Gruyère cheese, grated
Butter, for greasing
2 slices of good-quality roasted ham, chopped

Cook the macaroni in plenty of salted water until it still has a little bite to it – about 8–10 minutes. Put the cream into a saucepan, heat gently until reduced by half. Add the Parmesan and Gruyère and stir until they have melted. Remove from the heat.

Drain the pasta and put into a buttered ovenproof dish. Mix the chopped ham into the pasta and pour over the sauce. Scatter over more Parmesan and place under a hot grill for 3 minutes to crisp up the top and melt the cheese. Serve with a green salad.

Risotto with Black and White Truffles

175ml chicken stock, plus a little more, if needed (or use vegetable stock
   for a vegetarian option)
1 tbsp olive oil
1 shallot, peeled and finely chopped
60g risotto rice
Salt and freshly ground black pepper
1 small clove of garlic, peeled and crushed
½ glass of white wine
Grated Parmesan cheese
Generous knob of butter
A few very thin slices of bottled or fresh black truffle
Fresh white truffle, shaved, optional

Put the chicken stock into a small saucepan and gently heat. Keep hot and near.

Heat the olive oil in a heavy-based frying pan and cook the shallot until it is soft
and translucent. Add the risotto rice and stir to make sure each grain in coated in
the oil. Season with some salt. Add the garlic and wine and stir vigorously until it
has all evaporated.

Ladle in the stock and cook, little by little, stirring all the time until it is all used up
– this will take a good 15–20 minutes. Don't add more stock until the last lot has
been thoroughly incorporated. Taste the rice and make sure it is cooked.

When the liquid has nearly all been absorbed and the rice is tender but still has a
bit of a bite, take the pan off the heat and stir in the Parmesan, butter and a few
slices of the black truffle and a little juice from its bottle. Check the seasoning and
pour into a deep plate. Scatter over the shaved white truffle, if using, and serve
with a green salad.

MORE TIME

Meat and Poultry

Slow-cooked Lamb

Olive oil
1 lamb shank
1 banana shallot, peeled and quartered
1 carrot, peeled and cut into large chunks
½ clove garlic, peeled and crushed
¼ tsp chopped fresh rosemary
1 tsp plain flour
25ml red wine
100ml home-made lamb stock, or good store-bought chicken stock
1 sprig of thyme leaves
½ tsp mint jelly
Salt and freshly ground black pepper
½ tsp chopped fresh mint
A knob of butter

Preheat the oven to 190°C/375°F/gas mark 5.

Heat about 1 tablespoon of olive oil in a flameproof casserole dish. When it is sizzling, brown the lamb shank on all sides. Remove the shank, then brown the shallot, carrot and garlic. Stir in the flour to absorb the fat, then add the wine, stock, thyme and mint jelly.

Return the lamb to the pot and season with salt and pepper. Bring the lamb to the boil, cover with a lid and cook in the oven for 25 minutes, then reduce the heat to 150°C/300°F/gas mark 2 and continue to cook for another 45–60 minutes or until the meat is very tender.

Remove the lamb, shallots and carrots and cover and keep warm. Pour the liquid into a fat-separator jug, then pour just the meat juice back into the casserole, leaving the fat behind. Bring it to the boil and reduce for 5 minutes. Check the seasoning, then add the fresh mint and whisk in the knob of butter. Serve the lamb shank, carrot and shallot with the gravy and some mashed potato.

Steak Sandwich

Welsh rarebit:
15g butter
50g extra-mature English Cheddar cheese, grated
50ml Guinness or stout
1 tsp mustard powder
1 egg yolk, lightly beaten
1 tsp Worcestershire sauce
Salt and freshly ground black pepper

Sandwich:
1 rib eye steak, beaten out so that it is very thin
1 tbsp Welsh rarebit mix
2 slices of rye bread, toasted
Mustard, to serve

To make the Welsh rarebit, gently melt the butter in a saucepan. Add the cheese, stir, then add the stout slowly, stirring all the time until the mixture is smooth. Stirring constantly, add the mustard powder, egg yolk and Worcestershire sauce and heat until thick and glossy. Check the seasoning. Do not let the cheese mix boil or bubble or it will become lumpy. Set aside.

Preheat the oven to 200°C/400°F/gas mark 6. Line a small baking tray with Bake-O-Glide.

Heat up a grill pan until it is smoking. Season the steak with salt and pepper and cook to your liking, about 1–2 minutes each side. Set aside and keep warm.

Spread the Welsh rarebit mix on one piece of toast and place on the lined baking tray. Slide the tray into the oven for about 2 minutes or until it starts to bubble.

Remove the rarebit from the oven and put the steak on it, then top the steak with the second piece of toast. Serve with mustard and eat immediately. Any unused rarebit mix can be stored in the fridge until the following day (also see page 30).

Bolognese Sauce

This classic meat sauce can be used for stuffing cannelloni or a small marrow, as a base for chilli con carne, or simply served with spaghetti. Make it in this quantity and freeze in individual portions which will only take a matter of minutes to defrost. Makes 4 servings.

2 tbsp olive oil
1 medium sweet onion (red ones are fine), peeled and chopped
1 celery stalk, finely diced
1 small carrot, peeled and finely diced
350g minced beef
150g minced veal
150g minced pork
50g chicken livers, finely chopped
80ml red wine
200ml passata (sieved tomatoes)
250ml chicken stock
1 bay leaf
Salt and freshly ground black pepper
Grating of fresh nutmeg, optional, optional

Preheat the oven to 150°C/300°F/gas mark 2.

Heat the olive oil in a large ovenproof pan over a gentle heat, add the onion and soften for about 8–10 minutes – do not let it colour or burn. Add the celery and carrot and cook for a few minutes. Add the beef, veal and pork and cook for 8–10 minutes, breaking up any lumps with a wooden spoon. Add the chicken livers and cook for another few minutes.

Pour in the wine, passata and stock. Season with salt and pepper and add the bay leaf (and nutmeg and/or garlic, if using). Bring the pan up to a simmer, then transfer to the oven for 1½ hours, stirring every half hour or so. Check after 45 minutes to adjust cooking time. Do not cover. You should end up with a thick meaty sauce. Adjust the seasoning and serve or cool, then portion out into freezer bags and freeze.

Invite a friend over to do a big batch cook-in and split everything into small parcels and freeze - you will have a good time and lots of delicious food to eat.

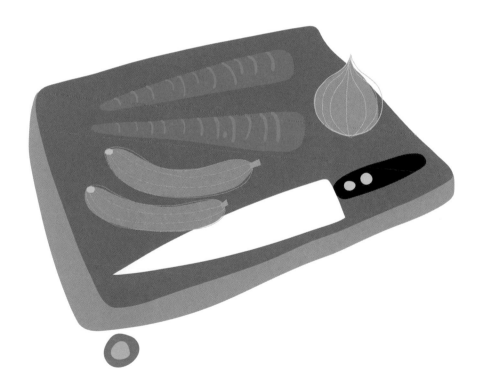

Baked Onion stuffed with Minced Meat

1 medium–large onion, peeled
Sunflower oil
A knob of butter
175g good-quality lean minced beef
1½ tsp tomato purée
1 clove of garlic, peeled and crushed
The leaves from 1 sprig of thyme
¼ tsp chopped fresh rosemary
Dash of Worcestershire sauce
Salt and freshly ground black pepper
1 rasher of streaky bacon

Preheat the oven to 200°C/400°F/gas mark 6.

Bring a pan of water up to brisk simmer, then plunge the onion in for about 5–8 minutes. Drain and leave until cool enough to handle. Cut the top off the onion and scoop out the inside of the onion, leaving an outer shell 2cm thick. Finely chop the onion you have removed. Butter the inside of the onion shell and place in the oven for 5 minutes, then remove and set aside. Reduce the oven temperature to 180°C/350°F/gas mark 4.

Heat 1 tablespoon of oil and the butter in a frying pan. Fry the chopped onion until it is just beginning to brown, then add the beef. When it has browned, add the tomato purée, garlic, thyme, rosemary and Worcestershire sauce and season with salt and pepper. Simmer for 5 minutes.

Spoon the meat into the onion shell. Wrap the rasher of bacon around the outside of the onion and secure in place with a wooden cocktail stick. Place the onion in a small ovenproof dish and bake for 25–30 minutes or until the bacon is cooked and the onion is soft. Serve with a green salad and boiled potatoes.

Beef Stroganoff

1–2 tbsp sunflower oil
A knob of butter
½ small onion, peeled and very thinly sliced
¼ tsp sweet smoked paprika, optional
10 button mushrooms, thinly sliced
75ml red wine
175g fillet of beef, cut into strips 6 x 2cm
1½ tsp plain flour
1½ tbsp brandy
2 tbsp double cream
2 tbsp sour cream
Sea salt and freshly ground black pepper

Use a large frying pan so you have room to fry the beef without steaming it.

Heat 1 tablespoon of sunflower oil and half the butter in the frying pan over a medium heat. Add the onions and fry until they are soft and translucent. Add the paprika, if using, and the mushrooms. Continue to cook for another minute. Pour in the red wine and cook for 3 minutes, or until you only have 2 tablespoons of liquor left. Remove the onion-mushroom mix to a bowl and set aside. (If you wish, the recipe can be cooked to this stage up to 6 hours in advance.)

Dust the beef strips in flour – simply put the flour on to a plate and dip the beef strips into it, shaking off the excess. Heat the remaining oil and butter in the same frying pan (no need to wash it) as hot as you can, and fry the beef very quickly so that it is still pink in the middle – this takes just a minute or so.

Transfer the beef to a warm plate, then deglaze the pan with the brandy and set it alight. When the flames have gone, add the onion-mushroom mix and heat through. Add the creams and season with salt and pepper. Taste. If the sauce is too thin, continue to cook it over a high heat to reduce. When it is ready, add the beef and stir to coat with the sauce. Serve with rice and a watercress salad.

Steak in Bloody Mary Marinade

For the best flavour, marinate this steak for at least 2 hours before cooking.

1 rib eye or fillet steak

Marinade:
2 tomatoes
Tabasco sauce, to taste
1 tsp Worcestershire sauce
1 tsp freshly grated horseradish
   (if you can't find fresh horseradish, use bottled)
Celery salt
15ml vodka
Dash of dry sherry

Using a mini food processor or stick blender, whiz together all the marinade ingredients. Check the seasoning. Pour the marinade into a zip-lock plastic bag, add the steak and leave to marinate for a minimum of 2 hours or overnight in the fridge. Turn the bag occasionally to coat the meat. Take the meat out of the fridge 30 minutes before cooking.

Heat a griddle pan until it is smoking. Drain the meat from the marinade (reserving the marinade) and place the steak on the very hot griddle pan. Cook for 2½–3 minutes on each side or until done to your liking.

In a saucepan, bring the marinade juices to a rapid boil, then simmer for 3–5 minutes. Check the seasoning. Serve the steak with the reduced marinade, a salad and a baked potato filled with sour cream and chives.

> *Marinating food overnight gives lots of flavour and tenderises meats too.*

Pork Chop with Oranges

This is best made with Seville oranges. When they are in season, make sure you freeze some to use later in the year.

Juice of ½ Seville orange, or if not in season juice of ¼ lemon
Juice of 1 orange
½ tsp crushed coriander seeds
1 thick pork chop, bone in
Salt and freshly ground black pepper
A little sunflower oil
Fresh coriander, to garnish
A slice of orange, to garnish

Put all the juice and the coriander seeds into a plastic bag, add the pork chop and marinate overnight.

When you are ready to cook, remove the chop from the marinade and pat dry with kitchen paper. Season with salt and pepper. Heat a little oil in a frying pan with a lid and brown both sides of the chop. Pour in the marinade, cover with the lid and cook for 10–12 minutes, depending how thick the pork is. Remove the chop to a plate and keep warm. Reduce the juices remaining in the pan down a little. To serve, pour the pan juices over the chop and garnish with the fresh coriander and orange slice. This goes well with mashed potato.

Lamb Cutlets in Puff Pastry

Sunflower oil
A knob of butter
1 shallot, peeled and finely chopped
2–3 button mushrooms, finely chopped
¼ tsp prepared garlic
2–3 fresh rosemary leaves, finely chopped
Salt and freshly ground black pepper
Packet of puff pastry (you will only need to use a ¼ of a packet,
  but the remainder can be frozen)
2 lamb cutlets
1 egg yolk, beaten

Preheat the oven to 200°C/400°F/gas mark 6. Line a baking tray with
Bake-O-Glide.

Heat up a little oil and butter in a frying pan and cook the shallot until soft, then
add the button mushrooms, garlic and rosemary. Season with salt and pepper
and cook until soft and there is no more liquid left. Spoon into a bowl and cool.

Roll out the pastry into two squares. Trim the cutlets of any fat and have at least
2cm of bare bone at the top. Season the cutlets with salt.

Put a quarter of the mushroom mix into the centre of the pastry, then place
the cutlet on top diagonally so that the bare bone sticks out and add another
quarter of mushroom mix on top of the cutlet. Fold and pinch the pastry around,
damping the edges with water to seal. Trim off any excess pastry. Repeat with the
remaining cutlet. Place the cutlets on the baking tray, seam side down, and brush
with beaten egg yolk. Bake for 20–25 minutes or until the pastry is golden. Serve
with French beans and carrots.

Venison Steak with Juniper Berries

This is a great dish but it does require a long marinating time.

175g fillet of venison
100ml sloe gin
1 small onion, peeled and chopped
¼ tsp prepared garlic
½ tsp fresh thyme leaves
½ tsp juniper berries, crushed
25g unsalted butter
1½ tbsp double cream
Salt and freshly ground black pepper

Put the venison into a plastic bag or non-metallic bowl. Pour over the sloe gin and add the onion, garlic, thyme and juniper berries. Ideally marinate for a minimum of 24 hours, or for as long as you can manage.

When you are ready to cook the venison, drain it from the marinade and set aside, reserving all the marinade. Also drain off the onions and set aside. What you want left are the drained onions and the marinade liquor.

Heat the butter in a frying pan. Fry the marinated onions until they are soft and starting to colour. Add the venison steak and fry for 2–3 minutes on each side. Remove the steak to a warm plate and leave to rest.

Deglaze the pan with the marinade and cook for 3–4 minutes. Stir in the cream, taste for seasoning and bring to the boil. Pour over the steak and serve with mashed potato.

Asian Seared Beef Salad

This dish is a fabulous mix of sweet and sour. Serve warm or at room temperature.

1 sirloin steak, about 175g
Sunflower oil
Sea salt
Handful of rocket
A small bunch of fresh mint leaves, striped from their stalks
A smaller bunch of fresh coriander
1 small kaffir lime leaf, tough centre vein removed and very thinly sliced
7cm piece of cucumber, peeled, seeded and cut into matchsticks
3–5 radishes, thinly sliced or cut into short matchsticks
Sliced tomatoes, to serve

Dressing:
1 bird's eye chilli, seeded and very finely chopped
1 juicy lime
½ tsp golden caster sugar
1½ tbsp Thai fish sauce
1 tbsp sweet chilli sauce

Rub the steak with a little oil and rub in some salt. Set aside until ready to cook.

To make the dressing, put the chilli, juice of the lime, sugar, fish sauce and sweet chilli sauce in a bowl and mix well. Taste and adjust with more of any of the ingredients until you get the balance right.

Heat a griddle pan so that it is smoking hot. Cook the steak for about 2½ minutes on each side. The meat should be pink inside, not overcooked. Transfer to a warm plate and wrap tightly with clingfilm.

Put the rocket, herbs, lime leaf, cucumber and radish into a large bowl. Cut the beef into strips. If there is any beef juice on the plate, add it to the dressing. Add the beef to the salad, pour on the dressing and toss well. Serve with sliced tomatoes.

Spare Ribs with Ginger, Chillies and Garlic

500g pork spare ribs

Marinade:
3cm piece of fresh ginger, peeled and grated
1 clove of garlic, peeled and crushed
1 tbsp honey
1 tbsp hoisin sauce
¼ tsp Chinese 5-spice powder
½ tsp dried chilli flakes
½ tbsp soy sauce
1 tbsp soft brown sugar
1 tsp Chinese rice wine

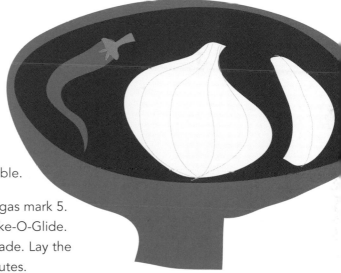

Mix all the marinade ingredients together in a non-metallic bowl. Add the ribs and marinate for a minimum of 1 hour, longer if possible.

Preheat the oven to 190°C/375°F/gas mark 5. Line a shallow roasting tin with Bake-O-Glide. Drain the ribs, reserving the marinade. Lay the ribs in the tin and bake for 15 minutes.

Pour the marinade into a saucepan and bring to the boil. When the ribs have been in the oven for 15 minutes, pour the sauce over them. Turn the heat down to 160°C/325°F/gas mark 3 and continue cooking for another 20–30 minutes or until the meat is tender. Serve hot with lots of napkins!

Calves' Sweetbreads in a Cream Sauce

Sweetbreads require a long soaking time, making this an ideal weekend recipe.

A pair of calves' sweetbreads
  (available from good supermarkets or butchers)
2–3 tbsp sunflower oil
50g butter
1 small onion, peeled and sliced
50g button mushrooms, sliced
2 tbsp white wine
100ml double cream
Salt and freshly ground black pepper
1½ tbsp plain flour

Soak the sweetbreads in cold water, changing the water frequently until there is no blood in the water. This may take up to 4 hours.

When they are ready to cook, put them in a saucepan of cold water. Bring to the boil and poach for about 2 minutes. Rinse under cold water and drain well. Dry the sweetbreads and remove all the membranes and any skin.

Heat up a little of the oil and butter in a pan and gently fry the onions until soft and translucent, then add the mushrooms and fry. Remove them to a warm dish and drain off any excess fat from the pan. Deglaze the pan with the white wine, then add the cream. Bring to a simmer and reduce for 3 minutes. Season with salt and pepper. Set aside.

Tip the flour onto a flat plate and season with salt and pepper. Dip the sweetbreads into the seasoned flour and shake off the excess. Heat up the rest of the oil and butter in a clean frying pan and gently fry the sweetbreads until they are golden on each side. Drain them on kitchen paper. Reheat the cream sauce and serve with the sweetbreads.

Rack of Lamb with Basil Cream

Sunflower oil
3-rib rack of lamb, chined and French trimmed
   (you will need to buy this from a butcher)

Basil cream:
20g butter
½ clove of garlic, peeled and crushed
2 shallots, peeled and finely chopped
1 tsp white wine vinegar
100ml double cream
Bunch of fresh basil
Bunch of fresh mint
A little salt

Preheat the oven to 190°C/375°F/gas mark 5.

Heat the oil in a roasting tin or ovenproof frying pan and seal the lamb over a
high heat. Transfer the tin or pan to the oven and cook for 5–8 minutes, depending
on how you like your lamb cooked. Remove from the oven and transfer the meat
to a warm plate. Cover with clingfilm and leave to rest for 5 minutes

To make the basil cream, melt the butter in a saucepan. Add the garlic and
shallots and gently cook for 3–5 minutes until soft but not coloured. Add the
white wine vinegar and deglaze the pan. Add the cream, basil and mint and cook
to reduce by half. Taste and season. Blitz the sauce in a mini food processor or
with a stick blender and keep warm. Serve with the lamb.

Potted Chicken

75g clarified butter made with unsalted butter, plus extra for sealing
(about 200g)
Blade of mace
Good grating of nutmeg
Pinch of cayenne pepper
Salt and freshly ground black pepper
150g cooked chicken meat – a mix of white and dark meat, shredded
(turkey also works well)
1½ tsp finely chopped fresh parsley

Put the clarified butter and spices into a bowl set over a pan of simmering water and melt over a gentle heat. Leave to infuse for at least 1 hour or more. Remove any large pieces of spice, like the blade of mace.

Preheat the oven to 160°C/325°F/gas mark 3.

Gently stir the shredded chicken and parsley into the spiced butter and spoon into a ramekin, leaving room for the clarified butter seal.

Place the ramekin in an ovenproof saucepan and pour in enough boiling water to come halfway up the side of the ramekin. Bring to the boil, then transfer to the oven for 25 minutes. Remove the ramekin and allow to cool.

Melt more clarified butter and pour over the top of each ramekin to seal. Refrigerate until ready to serve. Remove from the fridge 20 minutes before eating. Serve with warm toast.

Keep a few pots of fresh herbs on the windowsill for adding to dishes.

Thai Green Curry

You can make the sauce in advance and marinate the chicken in the morning for cooking that evening.

1 tbsp grapeseed oil
1 shallot, peeled and finely chopped
½ lemon grass stalk, finely sliced
1 clove of garlic, peeled and crushed
1 spring onion, trimmed
Zest and juice of 1 lime
¼ tsp coriander seeds, roasted and ground
¼ tsp ground cumin
4cm piece of fresh ginger, peeled and grated
½ red chilli, seeded and thinly sliced
1 tsp Thai fish sauce
3 basil leaves
1 tbsp chopped fresh coriander
1 tsp peanut butter
½ can coconut milk
1 chicken breast and 1 thigh, skinned, boned and cut into pieces
1 tsp chopped cashews, to garnish

Heat up a large wok and add the oil. Quickly fry, in this order, the shallot, lemon grass and garlic. Add all the remaining ingredients, except the coconut milk, cashews and chicken. Take the wok off the heat, then pour in the coconut milk. Let the sauce cool.

Put the chicken into a non-metallic bowl. Pour the sauce over the chicken, cover with clingfilm and marinate for a minimum of 2 hours – the longer, the better.

Preheat the oven to 200°C/400°F/gas mark 6. Transfer the chicken and marinade to an ovenproof dish and cook for 10–12 minutes. Stir, then cover with foil and cook for another 5 minutes. The coconut milk will probably split but it won't affect the taste. Garnish with more herbs and cashew nuts and serve with jasmine rice.

Chicken Thighs
with Coconut and Almonds

2 chicken thighs, skinned
1 tbsp grapeseed oil
1 shallot, peeled and finely chopped
1 small lemon grass stalk, finely sliced
¼ tsp prepared garlic
1 spring onion, trimmed and chopped
Juice and zest of ½ lime
¼ shredded kaffir lime leaf
Pinch of ground coriander
Pinch of ground cumin
¼ tsp prepared ginger
1 tsp Thai fish sauce
½ tbsp chopped fresh coriander
100ml coconut milk
½ tbsp toasted flaked almonds

Preheat the oven to 190°C/375F/gas mark 5. Put the chicken into an ovenproof dish and set aside.

Heat up a wok and add the oil. Next quickly fry, in this order, the shallot, lemon grass and garlic, then add everything else except for the coconut milk and flaked almonds. Take the wok off the heat, then pour in the coconut milk. Pour the sauce over the chicken.

Cook the chicken for 25 minutes or until it is cooked through (the juices run clear when the chicken thighs are pierced with a knife). The coconut milk will probably split but it won't affect the taste. Garnish the chicken with the almonds and serve with jasmine rice.

Italian Sausages
with Grilled Pepper and Onion

1 tbsp olive oil
½ red onion, peeled and sliced into strips
1 red pepper, sliced into strips
½ clove of garlic or ½ tsp prepared garlic
Pinch of sugar
Salt and freshly ground black pepper
2 good-quality Italian sausages

Heat the olive oil in a frying pan, then toss in the onion, red pepper, garlic and sugar and cook very gently over a medium heat until the onions are deliciously caramelised and thick – this will take about 8 minutes. Season with salt and pepper.

Meanwhile, cook the sausages in another frying pan on the hob or under a grill for 10 minutes or until they start to brown and are cooked through. Add the sausages to the onions and peppers and cook for a further minute, then spoon on to a plate and serve with crusty bread to mop up all the juices.

Chicken and Lobster Salad

1 chicken breast
1 bay leaf
Slice of onion
3 peppercorns
1 small carrot
1 sprig of fresh flat-leaf parsley
Dash of Tabasco sauce
Small dash of brandy
Squeeze of lemon juice
Salt and freshly ground black pepper
1 cooked lobster tail – you technically only need half a lobster tail,
   so save the other half for the next day if you aren't feeling piggy!
Iceberg lettuce, to serve

Mayonnaise:
1 large egg yolk
1 tsp Dijon mustard
2 tbsp white wine vinegar or lemon juice
Salt and freshly ground black pepper
150ml sunflower or vegetable oil
25ml extra virgin olive oil

First, make the mayonnaise. Whisk the egg yolk with the mustard, half the vinegar and a little salt and pepper until it starts to thicken – this will take 1–2 minutes. Combine the oils and add 1 teaspoon to the egg mixture at a time, whisking constantly. When it starts to thicken, you can add the oil more quickly but be very careful. It will take about 10 minutes to make the sauce by hand. When all the oil has been incorporated and you have a good thick mayonnaise, add the remaining vinegar and adjust the seasoning. Set aside.

Put the chicken into a saucepan and cover with cold water. Add the bay leaf, onion, peppercorns, carrot and parsley and bring up to a rapid simmer. Simmer for 4–5 minutes until the chicken is cooked. Drain and cool.

Season 1 tablespoon of the mayonnaise with the Tabasco, brandy, lemon juice, salt and pepper. To assemble the salad, chop up the lobster tail and the chicken and fold into the mayonnaise. Serve on chopped iceberg lettuce with granary bread.

The remaining mayonnaise can be stored, covered, in the fridge for 3 days.

Roasted Quail
with Rosemary and Quince

1 small red onion, peeled
30g quince cheese
1 quail, not trussed (partridge also works well)
Salt and freshly ground black pepper
1 tbsp soft butter
2 sprigs of fresh rosemary
1 tbsp plain flour
125ml good-quality chicken stock

Preheat the oven to 200°C/400°F/gas mark 6.

Cut the onion into thick slices and lay them on the bottom of a roasting tin. Put the quince cheese into the quail cavity and season with salt and pepper. Smear the butter over the bird and season. Put the quail on top of the onions and tuck in one of the rosemary sprigs. Roast for 15–20 minutes or until the juices run clear when the thigh is pierced with a skewer.

Remove the bird from the oven and carefully tip it so that any quince cheese left in the cavity runs into the pan juices. Transfer the quail to a warmed plate, cover with foil and leave to rest while you make the gravy.

Skim off any excess fat from the roasting tin, leaving about a tablespoon behind, then whisk in the flour until it is absorbed. If you prefer thinner gravy, add less flour. Add the stock little by little and bring to the boil, then let it simmer for 2–3 minutes. Chop the remaining rosemary leaves very finely. Strain the gravy into a warmed jug and add the rosemary.

Serve the quail with the gravy. Keep the vegetables light, such as French beans and a few small roasted potatoes.

Duck with Apples, Cranberries and Oranges

3 orange slices (use a Seville orange if possible)
3 apple slices
1 duck breast, scored
75ml game stock
25g fresh cranberries
Pinch of caster sugar
Salt and freshly ground black pepper

Preheat the oven to 200°C/400°F/gas mark 6.

Heat a non-stick frying pan. Place the duck in it, fat side down, and brown for 2 minutes, then turn over and brown the other side for a further minute or two.

Arrange the orange and apple slices in a roasting tin. Place the duck breast on top and cook for 15 minutes depending on how well done you like your duck. When ready, remove it from the tin and allow to rest for 5–10 minutes.

Drain off all the fat from the tin, but reserve it for a later use. Place the tin and its juices over a low heat. Deglaze the tin with the stock and add the cranberries and sugar, then bring to a rapid simmer. When the cranberries start to burst, remove the tin from the heat and taste. Season with salt and pepper.

Carve the duck and serve with the sauce and a few orange slices and some mashed potato.

Roast Grouse with Orange and Juniper

1 organic orange
4 juniper berries
1 oven-ready grouse, not trussed
Salt and freshly ground black pepper
1 red onion, peeled and thickly sliced
15g butter, softened
2 sprigs of fresh rosemary
½ tbsp plain flour
125ml good-quality chicken stock
Slice of French bread
Oil, for frying

Preheat the oven to its highest setting.

Using a potato peeler, shave the zest from the orange, leaving behind as much of the white pith as possible. Set aside. Cut the orange in half and squeeze the juice into a bowl and reserve for later.

Crush two of the juniper berries with a pestle and mortar and put them into the cavity of the grouse with one orange half and some salt and pepper.

Place the onion slices on the bottom of a roasting tin and scatter over half of the orange zest. Smear the butter over the grouse and season the outside of the grouse. Lay the grouse on the onions and tuck in one of the rosemary sprigs. Scatter in the remaining juniper berries.

Roast the grouse for 15–20 minutes or until the juices run clear when the thigh is pierced with a skewer. Remove the bird from the oven. Lift out the bird and carefully tip it so that any juices left in the cavity go into the pan juices. Move to a warmed plate, cover with foil and allow to rest while you make the gravy.

Skim off almost all excess fat from the tin, leaving about a tablespoon behind and whisk in the flour until it is absorbed. If you prefer thinner gravy, add less flour. Stir in the stock little by little and add the reserved orange juice. Bring to the boil, then let it simmer for 2–3 minutes. Chop the remaining rosemary leaves very finely. Strain the gravy into a warmed jug and add the rosemary.

To make the croûton, fry the slice of French bread in a little oil. Serve the grouse on this croûton with the gravy. Scatter over the remaining orange zest for garnish and serve with glazed carrots and mashed potato.

Duck in Green Peppercorn Sauce

1 duck breast, skin on
2 shallots, peeled and finely chopped
150ml red wine
2 tbsp good-quality chicken stock (or duck stock)
A knob of butter
1 tsp green peppercorns, drained and crushed
2 tbsp double cream
Salt

Score the skin on the duck breast and fry it in a hot frying pan for a few minutes until it is crisp and brown, then turn over and cook for a further 4–5 minutes, depending how rare you like the meat. Transfer to a warm plate and keep warm.

Drain off all but 1 teaspoon of the fat (reserve the fat as it is great in other recipes). Add the shallots to the pan and fry until very soft, then pour in the wine and continue to cook until it has reduced by half. Add the stock and cook for another 2 minutes. Whisk in the butter, then add the green peppercorns and cream. Add salt to taste.

Slice the duck breast on the diagonal and arrange on a plate. Pour over the sauce. Serve immediately with rosti potato and purple sprouting broccoli.

Pheasant with Walnuts and Madeira

1 tbsp clarified butter
1 pheasant breast
½ rasher of smoked bacon, chopped
½ onion, peeled and roughly chopped
1½ tsp chopped walnut
30ml Madeira
100ml game or chicken stock
Salt and freshly ground black pepper
1½ tsp crème fraîche

Preheat the oven to 180°C/350°F/gas mark 4.

Heat the clarified butter in a small casserole and brown the pheasant, then remove to a plate. Add the bacon and onion to the casserole and cook until lightly browned. Add the pheasant, scattering over the walnuts. Pour in the Madeira and enough stock to cover the meat, season and bring to the boil, then transfer to the oven and cook for 25 minutes.

When you are ready to serve, swirl in the crème fraîche and serve with polenta or mashed potato.

LESS TIME
Fish and Seafood

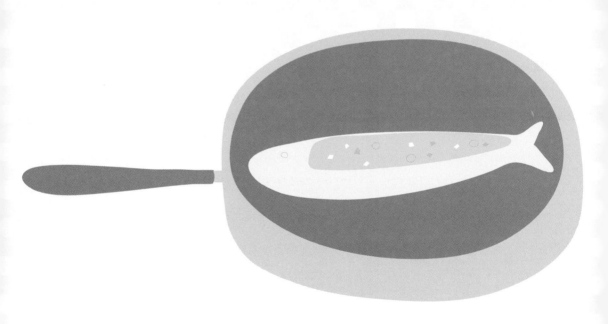

Moules Marinières

1kg fresh mussels
1 tbsp sunflower oil
50g butter
2 large shallots, peeled
2 cloves of garlic, peeled and chopped finely
100ml white wine
50ml double cream
Salt and freshly ground black pepper
Large bunch of fresh flat-leaf parsley, chopped

First deal with the mussels. Clean them in cold running water and pull off their beards – the stringy bits that hang from them. Put them into a large bowl of cold water. Discard any cracked mussels. If any remain open after washing, tap them – if they still don't close, throw them away.

Heat the oil and butter in a large heavy casserole with a lid until really hot. Put the shallots, garlic, white wine and 50ml water into the casserole and simmer for about 5–7 minutes or until the onions are soft and the liquid has reduced a little. Do not let anything colour or burn. Drain the mussels, add to the casserole and bring up to the boil. Put the lid on the casserole and cook the mussels for about 3 minutes, shaking the pan from time to time.

Tip the mussels into a colander placed over a bowl, set aside and keep warm. Discard any mussels that have not opened. Pour the liquid from the mussels back into the casserole, add the cream and season with salt and pepper. Bring up to the boil for 2 minutes, then add the parsley and tip the mussels back in. Serve with lots of crusty bread.

Sardines with Celery and Pine Nuts

4 sardine fillets
1 tbsp red wine
Olive oil
Salt and freshly ground black pepper
½ tbsp pine nuts
1 celery heart, roughly chopped, including any leaves

Preheat the oven to 190°C/375°F/gas mark 5.

Line a shallow baking tray with Bake-O-Glide and lay the sardine fillets skin side down. Sprinkle over the red wine and a drizzle of olive oil. Season with salt and pepper and press on the chopped celery and the pine nuts. Cover with clingfilm and leave for 10 minutes in a cool place.

Bake the fish in the preheated oven for 5 minutes. Great served with sourdough bread and a tomato salad.

Langoustines with Garlic Butter Sauce

5 langoustines
About 2 tbsp butter, at room temperature
Salt and freshly ground black pepper
1 tbsp chopped fresh flat-leaf parsley
2 cloves of garlic, peeled and crushed
Olive oil

Preheat the oven to 220°C/425°F/gas mark 7, or as high as it will go. Place a large shallow baking tray in the oven to heat up.

Split the langoustines in half lengthways, using a sharp knife or scissors.

Combine the butter, salt, pepper, parsley, garlic and a splash of olive oil together in a bowl. Spread on to the langoustine halves. Place the langoustines onto the preheated tray and cook for 8–10 minutes. Serve straight away with crusty bread and a green salad.

Arbroath Smokie with Pernod and Crème Fraîche

Small knob of butter
Splash of sunflower oil
1 shallot, peeled and finely chopped
1 Arbroath Smokie, skinned, boned and flaked
½ tbsp Pernod
1 tbsp crème fraîche
Salt and freshly ground black pepper
The top of a fennel bulb, chopped
Rye bread, to serve

Heat the butter and oil in a large frying pan, add the shallot and cook until it is soft but not coloured. Add the fish and the Pernod. Cook for a few minutes, then add the crème fraîche and cook for a further 2 minutes. Sprinkle in the fennel top, stir, season and spoon into a warmed serving dish. Serve with rye bread.

Escalope of Salmon with Cream Sauce

1 escalope of salmon, 1.25cm thick and large enough to cover a dinner plate
Sprinkling of white or rosé wine
Lemon zest
Freshly ground black pepper

Cream sauce:
4 tbsp double cream
Sea salt
½ tsp horseradish sauce

Preheat the oven or grill to its highest setting. Line a shallow baking tray with Bake-O-Glide.

To make the sauce, put the cream and a pinch of salt into a saucepan and bring up to a boil. Turn the heat down and simmer until it is reduced by half. When it is ready, remove from the heat and stir in the horseradish sauce.

While the sauce is reducing, put the escalope on the baking tray and season with the wine, some lemon zest and a good twist of pepper. Cook the salmon in the oven or under the grill for 3 minutes. Put the salmon on a warmed plate and drizzle over the sauce. Serve immediately with a watercress salad.

Never throw away leftover wine - freeze it in small quantities (such as in an ice-cube tray or in freezer bags) and use in sauces.

Fried Squid with Tartar Sauce

50g plain flour, sifted
Salt and freshly ground black pepper
175g prepared squid, cut into circles
Olive oil
Wedge of lemon

Tartar sauce:
1½ tbsp mayonnaise
1 tbsp crème fraîche
1 spring onion or a wedge of red onion
2 cornichons
3 green olives
1 tsp fresh tarragon leaves
1 anchovy
Tarragon vinegar or lemon juice, to taste
Salt and freshly ground black pepper

To make the tartar sauce, whiz everything up in a food processor but not too finely as you want to retain some texture.

Put the flour into a bowl and season well with salt and pepper. Toss the squid rings into the flour and shake off any excess flour. Heat the oil in a deep frying pan and quickly fry the squid until crisp. Do not overcook or the squid will become rubbery. Drain on kitchen paper and serve with the tartar sauce and a wedge of lemon.

Spaghettini with Prawns, Garlic and Cherry Tomatoes

85g spaghettini
1–2 tbsp good-quality olive oil
1 clove of garlic, peeled and crushed
Pinch of dried chilli flakes
4 cherry tomatoes, cut in half
125g raw king prawns, unshelled
Salt and freshly ground black pepper
A few sprigs of fresh flat-leaf parsley

Cook the pasta in salted boiling water until it still retains a little bite.

While the pasta is cooking, heat up the olive oil in a medium-sized frying pan and cook the garlic and chilli flakes for 1 minute. Add the tomatoes, cook for another few minutes, then add the prawns and cook until the shells turn bright pink. Season with salt and pepper.

Drain the pasta and add to the frying pan, then tear in the parsley and toss well. Serve straight away.

Dover Sole with Lemon Butter

Sunflower oil
Salt
1 Dover sole, prepared by the fishmonger
A splash of delicious olive oil
Unsalted butter
1 unwaxed lemon

Turn the grill on to its highest setting. Place a heavy shallow baking tray under it to heat up. Preheat the oven to 200°C/400°F/gas mark 6.

When the tray is hot, remove it from the grill and drizzle over a little sunflower oil and salt. Lay the fish skin side down on it, then drizzle over some olive oil and dot with a little butter and salt. Put the tray into the oven and cook for about 10 minutes. Then return to the grill and cook for 2–3 minutes to crisp up.

To test if the fish is cooked, pull a little of the flesh away from the bone – it should flake away easily. If not, cook for another minute or so.

To serve, squeeze over the lemon juice and spread over more butter. Serve with new potatoes and green beans.

Scallops with Lemon, Black Olives and Capers

Olive oil
4 scallops
Splash of white wine
The zest of half a lemon and some juice
Salt and freshly ground black pepper
1 small tomato, seeded and chopped
3–5 black olives in olive oil, pitted and roughly chopped
1 tsp capers, rinsed

Heat up a frying pan until it is very hot, then add a little olive oil. Add the scallops and cook for 1–2 minutes on each side. Remove from the pan and keep warm.

Deglaze the pan with the white wine. Add the lemon zest and juice and an additional 1½ tablespoons of olive oil. Season with salt and pepper and add the tomato, black olives and capers. Put the scallops on a warm plate and pour over any juices, then spoon over the sauce. Serve with crusty bread.

Smoked Haddock with Crème Fraîche and Chives

175g piece of undyed smoked haddock
Milk
150ml crème fraîche
1 tbsp snipped fresh chives
Freshly ground black pepper
Knob of butter

Put the fish into a pan and add just enough milk to cover. Bring up to the boil and boil for 1 minute, then remove from the heat and leave the fish to cook in the cooling milk for 5–8 minutes. It is done when it pulls away from the bones easily and is opaque. Drain off the milk and discard. Place the haddock on a warm plate and keep warm.

Pour the crème fraîche into the same pan and heat until it is bubbling, then simmer for 2 minutes until it has reduced a little. Add the chives and black pepper to taste, whisk in the knob of butter, then pour over the fish. This is good served with green beans and new potatoes.

Salt and Pepper Prawns

30g sea salt
1 tsp Sichuan peppercorns
3–4 small dried chillies
1 tbsp rice flour
Peanut oil or sunflower oil, for frying
6–8 raw tiger prawns, peeled but with their tails left on (strips of chicken, sliced calamari or whole baby calamari also work well)

Put the sea salt, peppercorns and chillies into a hot frying pan and dry fry them for 2–3 minutes to release their oils and become fragrant. Whiz them in a blender briefly so they are just combined. It is not worth making less of the salt mix so store it in a jar with a tightly fitting lid and freeze if you aren't going to use it within a month.

Tip the rice flour on to a plate. Heat up the oil in a deep saucepan until it is very hot. Dust the prawns in the flour, making sure they are well coated, and deep-fry for 2 minutes or until they are golden.

Put them into a bowl, spoon over some of the seasoned salt and mix well. Serve them immediately and enjoy!

Crab Crostini

50g crabmeat
50g cream cheese
1 tsp mayonnaise
1 tsp breadcrumbs
A dash of soy sauce
Pinch of cayenne pepper
Salt and freshly ground black pepper
2 pieces of ciabatta bread, lightly toasted

Preheat the oven to 180°C/350°F/gas mark 4.

Mix together all the ingredients except the bread in a bowl and season. Spread on to the lightly toasted ciabatta bread. Place on to a shallow baking tray and bake for 8–10 minutes. Serve with a rocket salad.

Make salad dressing and keep in a spray bottle in the fridge. Spray onto crisp leaves - this way you won't drown them in oil.

Salmon with a Herb Crust

1 tbsp fresh breadcrumbs
1½ tbsp chopped fresh herbs of your choice
½ tbsp pancetta cubes
175g fillet of salmon
1 tbsp olive oil, plus a little extra for cooking
Salt and freshly ground black pepper

Preheat the oven to 200°C/400°F/gas mark 6. Place a shallow baking tray in the oven to heat up.

In a bowl mix together the breadcrumbs, herbs and pancetta. Spoon this on top of the salmon, pressing it on. Remove the tray from the oven and drizzle on a little olive oil and some salt. Place the salmon skin side down on the tray and cook in the oven for about 8 minutes, depending how thick the fish is. Serve with new potatoes and green beans.

Grilled Tiger Prawns

6 raw tiger prawns, shelled and deveined
A few thin slices of fennel and yellow pepper
3 radicchio leaves, torn into medium pieces
1 baby gem lettuce, cut into wedges
Crusty bread, to serve

Dressing:
Juice of 1 lemon
3 tbsp light olive oil
Sea salt, to taste
Freshly ground black pepper
1 tbsp chopped fresh flat-leaf parsley

In a bowl, whisk the ingredients for the dressing together until well combined.

Put the tiger prawns into a bowl, add 2 tablespoons of the dressing and toss well to coat.

Heat a ridged griddle pan until it is very hot. Cook the prawns in the grill pan for about 2 minutes each side (don't over-cook or they will be tough). Put the cooked prawns into a bowl and add the peppers and fennel. Deglaze the pan with the remaining dressing and pour over the prawns.

To serve, arrange the radicchio and baby gem lettuce on a plate and put the tiger prawn and pepper salad on top. Garnish with more flat-leaf parsley and serve with lots of crusty bread

Black Cab Kippers

The black cab drivers in London call February and March 'kipper season' as apparently that is all they can afford to eat during the quieter months!

100g flaked kipper, all bones removed
25g unsalted butter, softened
Freshly ground black pepper
50g fromage frais
1 tbsp double cream
1 anchovy
½ tsp caster sugar
A scraping of lemon zest (about 2 turns on the grater)
1½ tsp lemon juice, or to taste
Lemon wedge and sourdough toast, to serve

Put the kipper, butter, pepper, fromage frais, double cream, anchovy, sugar and lemon zest into the bowl of a mini food processor and blitz until smooth. Check the consistency – you want a smooth pâté, neither too loose nor too stiff. Check the seasoning (I like to add lemon juice at the end to taste, but this is optional).

Pour the mixture into a ramekin. Serve with a lemon wedge on the side and with hot sourdough toast.

Grilled Sea Bass with Caper and Orange Butter

1 orange
1 tbsp soft unsalted butter
1 tsp caper berries, rinsed and drained
Pinch of ground coriander
Salt and freshly ground black pepper
Olive oil
A few sprigs of fresh coriander
175g fillet of sea bass

Preheat the oven to 200°C/400°F/gas mark 6.

Grate the zest from half the orange. Cut three slices from the orange and set aside. Squeeze a little juice from the remaining orange.

Mash the butter with the capers, orange zest, a little juice and the ground coriander. Season with salt and pepper.

Lay a piece of foil on a small baking tray. Smear a little olive oil on the foil and lay the orange slices and the sprigs of fresh coriander on top. Top with the sea bass and smear the fish with the flavoured butter. Fold up the fish in a foil parcel and bake for 8 minutes. Serve with a watercress salad and couscous.

Crab and Chilli Linguini

100g cooked crabmeat, half brown and half white meat
Zest and juice of ½ unwaxed lemon
A generous glug of good-quality olive oil
½ small red chilli, finely sliced and seeded
1 tbsp chopped fresh flat-leaf parsley
1 clove of garlic, peeled and crushed, or 1 tsp prepared garlic
Salt and freshly ground black pepper
75g linguini
Freshly grated Parmesan cheese, to serve

Mix the crabmeat, lemon, olive oil, chilli, parsley, garlic, salt and pepper together in a bowl. At this point the mix should be quite loose (add more oil if necessary). Cover with clingfilm and set aside. If you wish, this stage can be done in advance and put in the fridge; when you are ready to use the crab mix, take it out of the fridge half an hour before using.

Bring a large pan of water to a rapid boil and add a good amount of salt. Cook the pasta according to the packet instructions and drain. Mix in the crab and serve with freshly grated Parmesan cheese and a rocket salad.

Chopped fresh parsley freezes well and it doesn't need defrosting.

Leeks Vinaigrette with Potted Shrimps

5 baby leeks, cleaned and trimmed
1 pot of potted shrimps, at room temperature
Brown bread, to serve

Dressing:
1 tbsp red wine vinegar
1 tbsp walnut oil
2 tbsp sunflower oil
Salt and freshly ground black pepper
½ tsp sugar
1 tsp Dijon mustard

Preheat the oven to 190°C/375°F/gas mark 5.

Make the dressing by whisking the vinegar, oils, salt, pepper, sugar and mustard together in a bowl.

Put the leeks into an ovenproof dish and pour over 2–3 tablespoons of the dressing. Cover the dish with foil and bake for 15 minutes or until they are tender. Remove the leeks from the oven and spoon over the potted shrimps. Serve with brown bread and black pepper.

Smoked Salmon Rosti

1 medium potato
125g smoked salmon
½ a lemon
Freshly ground black pepper
½ tbsp finely chopped fresh dill
1 tbsp melted butter
Sour cream or crème fraîche, to serve

Preheat the oven to 190°C/375°F/gas mark 5.

Peel the potato, grate with a coarse grater and soak the shreds in a bowl of ice-cold water for 5–10 minutes.

Shred the smoked salmon. Using a fine grater, grate a little lemon zest over the salmon and add a squeeze of juice and a grinding of black pepper. Set aside.

Drain the potatoes and squeeze out all excess water. If necessary, wrap the potato in a clean tea towel and squeeze. Mix the grated potato with the smoked salmon and chopped dill and season with more black pepper. Add the melted butter and mix really well so that everything is coated in the butter.

Heat a non-stick shallow frying pan until it is hot and press the mix into the pan to form a round, flat 'cake'. Cook for 5–8 minutes on each side or until it is golden brown and the potato is cooked. Finish it off in the oven for a further 5–8 minutes.

Serve warm with a dollop of sour cream or crème fraîche and more black pepper, and with blanched asparagus when in season.

MORE TIME
Fish and Seafood

Kedgeree

50g long-grain rice (the ready-to-cook pouches
   are perfect for this recipe)
Splash of sunflower oil
40g butter
½ onion, peeled and chopped
¼ tsp curry powder
150g smoked haddock, cooked and flaked
1 hard-boiled egg, cut into quarters
Salt and freshly ground black pepper
1½ tsp chopped fresh flat-leaf parsley

Cook the rice in salted water for about 10 minutes (or follow the directions on the rice packet). Drain and keep warm.

Heat the oil and butter in a frying pan and fry the onion for 1–2 minutes. Add the curry powder and continue to cook until the onion is soft. Add the rice to the onion and mix well, then fold in the smoked haddock and hard-boiled egg. Taste for seasoning and garnish with the parsley.

Thai-style Fish Cakes with Chilli Dipping Sauce

150g white crabmeat, well drained
50g cooked prawns, chopped
½ tbsp Thai fish sauce
A scraping of garlic, or ¼ tsp prepared garlic
A good grating of fresh ginger
½ bird's eye chilli, seeded and finely chopped
1 tsp chopped fresh coriander
Zest of 1 lime, plus a squeeze of juice
1 egg, beaten
1 tbsp plain flour
Sunflower oil, for frying
Chilli dipping sauce, to serve

Put the crabmeat, prawns, fish sauce, garlic, ginger, chilli, coriander, lime zest and juice into a bowl and fold together gently so that everything is well combined. Add a little of the egg to bind together, then shape the mixture into three cakes.

Heat up some sunflower oil in a frying pan until very hot. Dip the fish cakes into the flour, then fry for 1 minute on each side. Drain on kitchen paper and serve with a wedge of lemon and chilli dipping sauce.

Grilled Oysters with Champagne Sauce

6 oysters, opened and cleaned
Any juices from the oysters
1 glass of champagne – half for you and half for the sauce!
2 egg yolks
75g butter
1 tbsp snipped fresh chives

Preheat the grill to its highest setting.

Arrange the oysters on to a shallow baking tray and set aside.

Put the oyster juices, egg yolks and half the champagne into a heatproof bowl and whisk until just mixed, then set the bowl over a pan of simmering water and continue whisking, adding the butter a little at a time until the sauce is thick and glossy.

Spoon a little sauce over each oyster and grill them for 1–2 minutes. Scatter over the chives and serve with more champagne!

Grilled Lobster with Ginger Sauce

750g live lobster
50g clarified butter
Salt and freshly ground black pepper

Ginger sauce:
50g cold butter, cut into cubes
½ clove of garlic, peeled and crushed
2 shallots, peeled and finely chopped
3cm piece of fresh ginger, peeled and finely chopped
125ml white wine

Put the live lobster on a chopping board and insert the point of a sharp knife hard into the back of the head and push down to kill the lobster. Cut the lobster in half, straight down the middle of the back. Remove any green intestines. Crack the claws.

Preheat the grill to its highest setting.

Lay the lobster in the roasting tin and brush over a little clarified butter and season with a little salt and pepper. Grill the lobster for about 8 minutes or until the shell has turned bright red and the meat is opaque.

While the lobster is cooking, make the ginger sauce. Melt a small cube of the butter in a saucepan and gently cook the garlic, shallots and ginger for 3–5 minutes until soft but not coloured. Add the white wine and cook to reduce by half. Whisk in the remaining cold butter a little at a time, working on and off the heat so that it emulsifies and thickens. Taste and season. Push the sauce through a sieve into a bowl and keep warm.

When the lobster is ready, take the tail meat out of the shell, and remove the claw meat in one piece if you can. Arrange on a plate and serve with the ginger sauce. This goes well with basmati rice and a green salad.

Cold Curried Prawns

1½ tsp sunflower oil
1 shallot, peeled and finely chopped
1 tsp curry paste
¼ tsp prepared ginger
100ml passata
2 tbsp double cream
Dash of Tabasco sauce
Salt and freshly ground black pepper
1½ tsp mango chutney
1½ tsp mayonnaise
½ Granny Smith apple, grated
Squeeze of lime juice
200g cooked king prawns, shelled

Heat the oil in a saucepan and fry the shallot until soft, then add the curry paste, ginger, passata and cream. Bring to a rapid simmer and cook for a few minutes. Set aside and cool completely.

When it is cool, fold the Tabasco, salt, pepper, chutney, mayonnaise, grated apple and lime into the curry mix. Taste and adjust the seasoning. Fold in the prawns and serve with wild rice.

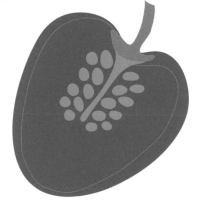

Fish and Chips

Oil, for frying
1 tbsp plain flour, seasoned with salt and pepper
175g piece of cod or haddock, skinned and boned

Batter:
115g plain flour, sifted
1 tsp baking powder
½ tsp salt
250ml sparkling ice-cold water or ice-cold beer

Chips:
2 potatoes, peeled and cut into strips – fat or thin, your choice
1 tbsp sunflower oil
Salt

First make the batter. Mix all the ingredients together in a large bowl, then leave to rest for 1 hour.

To make the chips, preheat the oven to 200°C/400°F/gas mark 6. Put a shallow baking tray in the oven to heat up.

Put the potatoes into a bowl. Spoon over the oil and mix really well so that all the potatoes are coated. Season with some salt. Tip the potatoes into the heated baking tray and cook for about 1 hour. Check them halfway through cooking time and turn them so that they become golden and crispy on all sides.

When the chips are nearly ready, heat up enough sunflower oil in a deep frying pan to cover the fish. Put the seasoned flour into a plastic bag, add the fish into the bag and coat with the flour. Remove the fish from the bag and dip into the batter, then fry in the heated oil until golden and crisp – about 3–4 minutes. Drain on kitchen paper and serve with the chips.

Grilled Scallops with Fennel and Hazelnuts

4 scallops in the shell – ask the fishmonger to loosen them
from the shell for you

Fennel butter:
1½ tbsp soft unsalted butter
1 tbsp finely chopped fennel fronds (the tops of fennel bulbs)
6 hazelnuts, roasted, skinned and chopped
Salt and freshly ground black pepper
Squeeze of lime juice

Mash the butter, fennel, hazelnuts, some salt and pepper and a squeeze of lime juice together. Cover and put in the fridge to chill.

Preheat the grill to its highest setting or preheat the oven to 190°C/375°F/gas mark 5.

Lay the scallops on a shallow baking tray. Cut the fennel butter into four pieces and place a piece on each scallop.

Cook under the grill or in the oven for 3–5 minutes or until just opaque. Serve with a green salad and basmati rice.

Mackerel with
Hummus and Pitta Bread

This will make more hummus than you need, but you can keep it in the fridge for up to 3 days.

Olive oil
1 fresh mackerel, cleaned, gutted and cut into two fillets
Salt and freshly ground black pepper
1 pitta bread
1 little gem lettuce, cut into quarters
1 ready prepared baby beetroot from a jar, drained and cut into cubes

Hummus:
1 tin of organic chick-peas in water (240g drained weight), drained but
   with some of the water reserved
1 large clove of garlic, peeled
1 tbsp tahini or smooth peanut butter
Juice and zest of 1 lemon
Salt and freshly ground black pepper
3–4 tbsp olive oil (choose something fruity but not too strong)

Reserve 1 tablespoon of the chick-peas to garnish. To make the hummus, plop everything except the oil into a food processor and whiz until smooth. If it is a bit thick, add some of the reserved chick-pea water. Slowly pour in the oil through the feeder at the top until the consistency is as you like it.

Heat up 1 tablespoon of olive oil in a frying pan and add the mackerel fillets, skin side down. Season with a little salt and pepper. Cook the mackerel for 2–3 minutes on each side.

Toast the pitta bread and slit open, leaving one end intact. Drizzle a little olive oil into the pitta bread and put in half the lettuce. When the mackerel is cooked, gently flake it and mix with about 2 tablespoons of the hummus, then spoon on to the lettuce. Add the beetroot and the remaining lettuce, pushing everything in tightly. Add the reserved whole chick-peas, more olive oil if you wish and season.

Cook a big batch of chick-peas and divide up into small bags and freeze for making hummus or adding to soups.

Brown Trout with Hazelnuts

1 tbsp plain flour
Salt and freshly ground black pepper
1 fresh trout, gutted and rinsed
50ml milk
A knob of butter
1 tsp sunflower oil
½ tbsp chopped fresh flat-leaf parsley
½ tbsp chopped roasted hazelnuts
Zest and juice of 1 lemon

Season the flour with some salt and pepper and spoon it on to a flat dish. Dip the trout into the milk, then into the flour and coat well shaking off the excess.

Heat the butter and oil in a large frying pan over a medium heat until frothing, then add the trout. Cook for 3–5 minutes on each side (add more butter if necessary) until crispy. Make sure the butter does not burn. Set aside on a serving dish and keep warm.

Add a little more butter, the parsley, hazelnuts, lemon zest and juice, salt and pepper to the pan and cook for 1 minute, then pour over the trout and serve.

Normandy Mussels

1kg fresh mussels
1 tbsp sunflower oil
50g butter
2 large shallots, peeled
1 clove of garlic, peeled and finely chopped
100ml cider
50ml crème fraîche
Salt and freshly ground black pepper
Large bunch of flat-leaf parsley, chopped
Crusty bread, to serve

Clean the mussels in cold running water and pull off their 'beards' – the stringy bits that hang from them. Put them into a large bowl of cold water. If any of the mussels are cracked or still open after they have been washed, tap them – if they still don't close, throw them away.

Heat up the oil and butter in a large, heavy lidded casserole until really hot. Put the shallots, garlic, cider and 50ml water into the casserole and simmer for about 5–7 minutes or until the shallots are soft and the liquid has reduced a little. Do not let anything colour or burn.

Drain the mussels and add to the casserole. Bring up to the boil, add the lid and, shaking the pan from time to time, cook the mussels for about 3 minutes.

Place a colander over a bowl and tip the mussels into the colander. Discard any mussels which have not opened. Set aside and keep warm. Pour the liquid from the mussels back into the casserole, add the crème fraîche and season with salt and pepper. Bring up to the boil for 2 minutes, then add the parsley and tip the mussels back in. Serve with lots of crusty bread.

Lobster Cocktail

1.5kg live lobster
Grapeseed oil
1 head of little gem lettuce

Dressing:
2 tbsp good mayonnaise (home-made is best – see page 78)
2 tsp tomato ketchup
Dash of Tabasco sauce
Dash of Worcestershire sauce
1 tsp brandy
Salt and freshly ground black pepper
A squeeze of lemon juice

Combine all the dressing ingredients in a bowl and whisk together. Taste and adjust seasoning. Set aside.

Preheat the oven to 220°C/425°F/gas mark 7.

Put the live lobster on a chopping board, insert the point of a sharp knife hard into the back of the head and push down to kill the lobster. Cut the lobster in half, straight down the middle of the back. Remove any green intestines. Crack the claws. Lay the lobster in a large roasting tin and drizzle over a little grapeseed oil. Roast for 10–15 minutes, then remove from the oven and allow to cool.

Take the lobster out of its shell, devein the tail and remove the claw meat in one piece, reserving to one side. Chop the lobster into cubes and in a large bowl combine the cubed lobster and 2–3 tablespoons of dressing and gently toss together. Arrange the lettuce leaves on a plate and spoon over the lobster and garnish with the reserved claws. Serve the remaining dressing on the side.

Crab Spring Rolls with Lemon Oil

You will have to buy a whole packet of spring roll pastry, but you can freeze any leftovers for another occasion. Start this recipe well in advance – the lemon oil needs to stand overnight.

Lemon oil:
1 unwaxed lemon
250ml grapeseed oil
2 lemon grass stalks

Spring rolls:
Sunflower oil
1 carrot, washed and grated
2cm piece of fresh ginger, peeled and grated
1 spring onion, trimmed and finely sliced
1 tsp chopped fresh coriander, plus extra for garnish
¼ bird's eye chilli, seeded and finely sliced
1½ tsp Thai fish sauce
½ tsp sesame oil
100g white crabmeat, cooked and shredded
1 packet of spring roll pastry
1 egg yolk, beaten, for egg wash
Salad leaves, to serve

First make the lemon oil. Cut the peel from the lemon and place in a saucepan. Split the lemon grass stalks and add to the pan. Pour over the oil, cover with clingfilm and leave at room temperature overnight.

Next day, bring the oil mix to the boil, then simmer for 10 minutes. Strain into a sterilised jar. The oil will last for about 1 month when stored in the fridge.

To make the spring roll filling, heat 1 teaspoon of sunflower oil in a frying pan. When very hot, quickly stir-fry the carrot, ginger, spring onion, coriander, chilli, fish sauce, sesame oil and crabmeat for 1–2 minutes.

Lay one sheet of pastry on a flat surface and brush with egg wash all around the edges. Put a teaspoon of the crab mix 4cm from the top of the pastry and fold the pastry tightly over the mix so that all the air is removed, carry on rolling it up and secure the end with a little more egg wash so that it acts as glue. Repeat to make about 3 spring rolls in total. (Any unused pastry can be frozen.)

Heat some more sunflower oil in a frying pan, add the spring rolls and shallow fry until brown and crispy on the outside. Serve them on a bed of salad with a little of the lemon oil drizzled over the top.

Potato Blinis with Smoked Salmon and Sour Cream

I always make a stack of these as they can be frozen. Reheat in a frying pan for 2–3 minutes. Makes 10–14 blinis, depending on size.

Blinis:
100g cold smooth mashed potatoes, made without any added butter or milk (I use a potato ricer to make them smooth)
1 egg, separated
1 tbsp double cream
1 rounded tbsp self-raising flour
Salt and white pepper
Sunflower oil

Topping:
Smoked salmon, cut into strips or chopped
Sour cream
Snipped chives
Freshly ground black pepper
Squeeze of lemon juice

In a large bowl mix together the potato, egg yolk, cream, flour and salt and pepper. Whisk the egg white in a separate bowl until stiff, then gently fold into the potato mix.

Lightly grease a non-stick frying pan with a piece of kitchen paper dipped in some sunflower oil. Drop spoonfuls of the blini mix into the frying pan. Cook for 1½ minutes on each side, turning carefully, then remove to a warmed plate.

For the topping, mix some sour cream with chives, smoked salmon strips, a squeeze of lemon juice and black pepper. Top each blini with a teaspoon of the mixture.

Potted Crab with Sourdough Toast

2–3 tbsp clarified butter, made with unsalted butter,
   plus more for sealing
Blade of mace
Generous grating of fresh nutmeg
Pinch of cayenne pepper
Generous grating of lemon zest
1 prepared crab (approximately 250g)
Salt and freshly ground black pepper
Sourdough toast, to serve

Put the clarified butter, spices and lemon zest into a small pan and melt over a gentle heat (or place in a heatproof bowl and melt in a microwave). Leave to infuse for at least an hour or more. Remove any large pieces of spice, such as the blade of mace.

Gently stir the crab into the spiced butter and pack into two ramekins, leaving room for the clarified butter seal.

Put the ramekins in a saucepan and pour in enough boiling water to come halfway up the sides of the ramekins. Bring to the boil for 2–3 minutes, then remove the ramekins from the pan and allow to cool. Melt more clarified butter and pour over the top of each ramekin to seal. Refrigerate until ready to serve.

Remove from the fridge 20 minutes before serving. Serve with hot sourdough toast or warm flat bread. Will keep in the fridge for up to 3 days.

LESS TIME
Vegetarian

Honeyed Pears with Gorgonzola and Thyme

1 really ripe pear
A little curly endive
50g Gorgonzola cheese
1 sprig of fresh thyme
1 tsp honey
1 tsp balsamic vinegar
A little olive oil
Salt and freshly ground black pepper
Sourdough toast, to serve

Peel and core the pear and slice into thick slices. Spread the curly endive on a plate and put the pear on top. Crumble over the cheese and scatter over the thyme leaves. Spoon over the honey, drizzle with the balsamic and olive oil, then season to taste.

Serve with sourdough toast. If you wish, you could also add some walnuts or cobnuts.

Gulls' Eggs with Asparagus Spears

Gulls' eggs and asparagus come into season at around the same time – gulls' eggs can only be harvested by licensed gatherers from April until early June. Expect to pay quite a lot for the eggs, but remember you will probably only have them once in the season. They can be served hard boiled or soft boiled, as in this recipe.

> 2 gulls' eggs
> 6 fat spears of asparagus
> Pinch of cayenne pepper
> ¼ tsp celery salt
> A little butter
> Thinly sliced brown bead and butter, to serve

Snap the asparagus spears near the woody end – they will naturally break where they are tough. Discard the woody ends.

Bring two pans of water up to the boil, one for the asparagus and a small one for the eggs – you don't want them to rattle around in the pan more than they have to.

When the water is boiling, cook the asparagus for 3–5 minutes and, in the other pan, the eggs for 4 minutes – depending on the size they may need less or more time so that they are soft boiled.

Mix the cayenne pepper with the celery salt and place on the serving plate. Put the eggs into two egg cups and the asparagus spears on the side with a little butter spread over the tips. Cut off the top of the egg and dip in the asparagus spears. Serve with thinly sliced brown bread and butter.

Hash Browns with Fried Onions and Mushrooms

You can add chopped cooked pancetta to this dish if you like a bit of meat!

1 large waxy potato, peeled but left whole
Sunflower oil or dripping
A knob of butter
1 small onion, peeled and chopped
3–4 field mushrooms, depending on size, sliced
Salt and freshly ground black pepper
1 egg

Cook the potato in boiling water for 3 minutes – you don't want it cooked all the way through. Remove from the water and cool.

Heat up a little oil and butter in a frying pan and cook the onion until slightly charred around the edges. Remove from the pan, then cook the mushrooms. Remove to a plate and keep warm.

Grate the potato into a bowl, add the cooked onion and season with salt and pepper. Mix together well. Heat up a little more oil and butter in the pan, add the potato mix and fry in either small rounds or one large one until crispy. Slide on to a warm plate and keep warm. Fry the egg in the same pan, then top the hash brown potato with the mushroom slices and the fried egg.

Gorgonzola and Mascarpone Pasta Bake

A knob of butter, plus extra for greasing
50g penne pasta
1 tomato, cut into thick slices
55g Gorgonzola cheese
1½ tbsp mascarpone cheese
Salt and freshly ground black pepper
15g Parmesan cheese, grated

Preheat the oven to 180°C/350°F/gas mark 4. Grease an ovenproof dish with a little butter.

Bring a pan of salted water up to the boil and cook the penne pasta until it still has a little bite to it. Drain.

Put the tomato slices on the bottom of the prepared dish. Mix the pasta with the Gorgonzola and mascarpone and the knob of butter. Season with a little salt and pepper – not too much as the Gorgonzola is salty. Spoon the mixture over the tomato, then scatter over the Parmesan. Bake for 20–25 minutes or until it is golden on top.

Cheddar Pudding

15g butter, melted, plus extra for greasing
1 slice of white bread, crusts removed
1½ tbsp white wine
1 egg
150ml milk
Salt and freshly ground black pepper
55g Cheddar cheese

Preheat the oven to 200°C/400°F/gas mark 6. Grease a small ovenproof dish with a little butter.

Cube the bread into the dish and pour over the wine and melted butter. Beat the egg with the milk and season with salt and pepper. Pour over the bread, then sprinkle over the cheese. Bake for 20–25 minutes or until it is risen and golden. Serve with a green salad.

Baked Egg with Spinach

Butter, for greasing
1 clove of garlic, peeled and impaled on the tines of a fork
1 handful of fresh spinach leaves, washed and trimmed
A grating of fresh nutmeg
Salt and freshly ground black pepper
2 tbsp double cream
1 large fresh egg
Buttered brown bread, to serve

Butter the inside of a ramekin and set aside.

Gently heat a small knob of butter in a small saucepan and rub the garlic around the inside of the pan, making sure it is firmly secured on the fork tines. Add the spinach to the pan and cook for just a few minutes until wilted. Add the nutmeg and season with salt and pepper, using the garlic fork to stir the spinach.

Squeeze out any excess liquid from the spinach and place in the base of the ramekin. Spoon over half the cream, then carefully break the egg on to the spinach and spoon over the remaining cream. Season again with salt and pepper.

Rinse out the small saucepan used for cooking the spinach. Put the ramekin into the pan and pour boiling water around the ramekin to come halfway up the side, taking care not to splash any water into the ramekin. Bring to the boil, cover the pan with a tightly fitting lid and gently simmer for 3–5 minutes or until the egg is just cooked.

Remove it from the water bath, and serve with brown bread and butter.

Pine Nut and Raisin Pilaf

1 tbsp olive oil
1 shallot, peeled and chopped
50g basmati rice
½ tbsp raisins
Pinch of saffron threads
½ tsp sea salt
1 tbsp pine nuts
1 large tomato, chopped
½ tbsp chopped fresh mint, plus whole leaves to garnish

Pour the oil into a saucepan with a tightly fitting lid and heat gently. Add the shallot and cook until softened. Add the rice, raisins, saffron and salt and stir to coat everything thoroughly in the oil and onion. Add 225ml cold water and bring to the boil. Place the lid on top and cook over a moderate heat for 20 minutes.

While the rice is cooking, put the pine nuts into a frying pan and dry fry them until they are brown and golden, then set aside. When the rice is cooked, fluff it up with a fork and place a clean tea towel over the pan to collect excess steam.

Stir in the pine nuts, tomato and mint and serve with a few large mint leaves on top for a garnish. Great served with a cucumber and mint salad.

Asparagus and Lemon Pasta

4 thick asparagus spears
50ml double cream
Zest and juice of 1 lemon
Generous knob of butter
Salt
100g tagliatelle
1 organic egg yolk, beaten
50g Parmesan cheese, grated, plus more for serving
Handful of fresh flat-leaf parsley, roughly chopped

First, sort out the asparagus. Take each spear and hold it between your two hands and bend it – the spear will snap at the natural woody point so there is no guess-work involved when trimming it. Tidy the ends with a knife if necessary.

Bring a large shallow pan of water up to the boil. Cook the asparagus spears in the boiling water for 3–5 minutes or until they are tender, but don't overcook them. Drain and cut into bite-sized pieces and set aside.

Gently warm the cream in a saucepan, then add the lemon zest, juice and butter. Remove from the heat and set aside.

Bring a pan of water to a rapid boil and add a generous amount of salt to the water. Cook the pasta according to the instructions and drain.

Pour the lemon sauce over the drained pasta and stir in the egg yolk, then fold in the asparagus, Parmesan and parsley. Serve straight away.

Baked Eggs with Black Truffle

Butter, at room temperature
Salt and freshly ground black pepper
3 fresh truffle shavings
2 'truffled' eggs (see page 154)
1 tbsp double cream
Bread, to serve

Preheat the oven to 180°C/350°F/gas mark 4. Place a baking tray in the oven to heat up.

Butter the inside of a small, flat ovenproof dish and sprinkle with salt and pepper. Put one slice of the truffle on the bottom of the dish. Break the eggs into the dish. Pour over the double cream and set the dish on the hot baking tray. Slide the tray into the oven and bake for 5–8 minutes. Remove from the oven, scatter over the remaining truffle shavings and serve with warm bread.

Eggs Florentine

    2 really fresh eggs
    200g spinach
    Butter, for greasing
    2–3 tbsp ready-made cheese sauce
    25g Gruyère cheese, grated
    1 tsp breadcrumbs
    Melba toast, to serve

Preheat the grill to its highest setting.

Cook the spinach in a little butter in a frying pan over a medium heat. Remove, drain well and chop. Butter a shallow ovenproof dish and put the spinach on the bottom.

Poach the eggs in a pan of simmering water for about 2½–3 minutes. Drain and place on top of the spinach. Spoon over the cheese sauce and sprinkle over the cheese and breadcrumbs. Place under the grill until brown. Serve with Melba toast.

Goats' Cheese Soufflé Pudding

Butter, for greasing
50g Parmesan cheese, plus more for topping
100g goats' cheese or other crumbly cheese
2 large eggs, separated
2 tbsp double cream
1 sprig of fresh thyme, leaves stripped from stalk
Salt and freshly ground black pepper

Preheat the oven to 200°C/400°F/gas mark 6. Butter a shallow ovenproof dish.
Sprinkle with a little of the Parmesan, swirling it around to coat the inside of
the dish, then tip out and reserve the excess cheese. Place the dish in the freezer
to chill.

Beat the goats' cheese with the egg yolks and cream, then add the reserved
Parmesan and thyme. Season with salt and pepper. Whisk the egg whites until
they are stiff but still soft, then gently fold into the egg yolk mixture so that
everything is combined.

Pour the mixture into the prepared dish and scatter over some more Parmesan.
Place on a baking tray. Bake the soufflé for 10–15 minutes until golden on top.
Test if it is ready by inserting a knife point at the centre – if it is still a little runny,
return to the oven. Serve with a green salad.

Endive Salad with Manchego Cheese and Fried Quails' Eggs

The heart of a curly endive
1 generous slice of chewy sourdough bread
50g Manchego cheese, crumbled
Olive oil, for frying
2–3 quails' eggs

Dressing:
2 tbsp groundnut oil
1 tbsp hazelnut oil
1 tbsp mild white wine vinegar
1 tsp honey
1 tsp Dijon mustard
Salt and freshly ground black pepper

To make the dressing, simply whisk together all the ingredients and set aside.

Separate the endive leaves and put into a bowl. Spoon over 2 tablespoons of dressing and toss well (unused dressing can be stored in the fridge in a covered container for a couple of days).

Toast the bread and place on a plate. Put the endive onto the toast and top with the crumbled cheese.

Heat the olive oil in a non-stick frying pan. Using a serrated knife, carefully cut open the quails' eggshells and drop the eggs into the pan. Fry them in the oil, basting a little. They will take about 30 seconds to cook. Top the salad with the eggs and spoon over a little more dressing.

Pasta with Fresh Tomato and Basil Sauce

100g pasta (any shape you like)
Grated Parmesan cheese, to serve

Sauce:
1 tbsp olive oil
4 really ripe tomatoes, roughly chopped
Grating of garlic or ¼ tsp prepared garlic
Pinch of sugar
Splash of balsamic vinegar
Salt and freshly ground black pepper
4–5 fresh basil leaves

Pour the olive oil into a heavy saucepan and heat up with the tomatoes, garlic, sugar, balsamic vinegar and season with salt and pepper. Cook very gently over a medium heat so that it becomes thick – this will take around 5 minutes. Taste and season again. Remove from the heat, add 3 basil leaves to the sauce and stir well, then push through a sieve. Set aside.

Bring a pan of salted water up to the boil and cook the pasta according to the directions on the packet. Drain well, then add the sauce to the pasta. Tear in the remaining basil, stir well and serve with Parmesan cheese.

Spaghetti Pangrattato

The pangrattato are breadcrumbs and provide a crunchy contrast to the soft pasta.

> 80g spaghetti
> 2 tbsp fresh tomato sauce
> 6 black olives, stoned and roughly chopped
> 1 tbsp freshly grated Parmesan cheese
> Salt and freshly ground black pepper
> Good-quality olive oil
> 1 tbsp toasted breadcrumbs made from ciabatta bread

Cook the pasta according to the packet instructions and drain, leaving a little cooking water with the pasta.

Heat up the fresh tomato sauce in a pan and toss in the drained pasta, leaving behind the cooking water. Add the olives and Parmesan, then season with salt and pepper. Transfer to a warm serving bowl, add a slick of olive oil and top with the toasted breadcrumbs.

Spaghetti with Broad Beans and Pecorino

About 10 broad beans
100g spaghetti
Salt
2–3 tbsp olive oil
2 shallots, peeled and finely chopped
½ clove of garlic, peeled and crushed, or 1 tsp prepared garlic
Handful of fresh flat-leaf parsley, roughly chopped, plus extra for serving
Generous knob of butter
Grated Parmesan cheese, plus extra for serving
15g pecorino cheese

To prepare the broad beans, shell them, then blanch in rapidly boiling water. Drain the beans, then plunge them into ice-cold water for a minute or two. Pop each bean out of its pale green skin by pinching with thumb and forefinger.

Bring a large pan of salted water up to the boil and cook the spaghetti until it is still has a little bite to it.

While the pasta is cooking, heat the olive oil in a large frying pan and soften the shallots. Add the garlic, parsley and a splash of the pasta water and gently cook over a medium heat.

Drain the pasta, reserving a little of the cooking water, and add the pasta to the onion mix. Toss in the broad beans and season with salt and pepper. Add the butter and gently stir so that the pasta is thoroughly coated, adding a little of the reserved water if it is too dry. Crumble in the cheese and add a little more parsley. Check the seasoning and adjust to taste.

Portobello Mushrooms with Melted Brie

2 Portobello mushrooms, stalks removed
Olive oil
Salt and freshly ground black pepper
A knob of butter
1 shallot, peeled and finely chopped
Handful of mixed wild mushrooms, left whole if small or
    cut in half or smaller if very large
1 small clove of garlic, peeled and crushed
1 tbsp chopped fresh flat-leaf parsley
1 tbsp crème fraîche
2 slices of good-quality Brie
Crusty bread, to serve

Preheat the oven to 190°C/375°F/gas mark 5.

Lay the Portobello mushrooms on a shallow baking tray, drizzle over some olive oil and season with salt and pepper. Bake for about 8 minutes or until they are just soft.

Meanwhile, heat up a little olive oil and the knob of butter in a frying pan. Cook the shallot until soft, then add the wild mushrooms, garlic, most of the parsley, salt and pepper. Don't let the garlic burn. After 5–8 minutes, when the mushrooms are tender, stir in the crème fraîche and simmer for 2 minutes to let the sauce thicken.

Take the Portobello mushrooms out of the oven. Spoon the wild mushroom mix on to the Portobello mushrooms and sprinkle over a little more chopped parsley. Top with the slices of Brie and return to the oven for a few minutes so that the Brie just starts to melt. Serve with crusty bread.

Penne Pasta with Taleggio Cheese

Butter, for greasing
75g penne pasta
6 cherry tomatoes, cut in half
1 tsp chopped fresh flat-leaf parsley
Salt and freshly ground black pepper
4 slices of Taleggio cheese
1 tbsp grated Parmesan cheese

Preheat the oven to 180°C/350°F/gas mark 4. Butter a shallow ovenproof dish.

Cook the pasta according to the instructions on the packet. Drain and mix through a little butter, the tomatoes, parsley, salt and pepper. Pour into the prepared dish, lay the Taleggio on top and scatter over the Parmesan. Bake for 15 minutes or until bubbling and golden. Serve with a green salad.

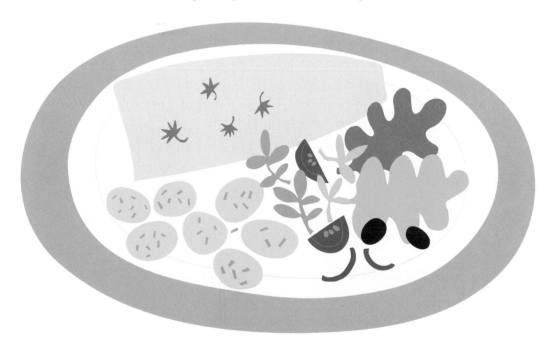

Spaghetti with Garlic and Olive Oil

This is real comfort food!

80g dried spaghetti
1 clove of garlic, peeled and crushed
2 tbsp the best olive oil you can find
Salt and freshly ground black pepper

Cook the pasta in salted boiling water until it still has a little bite.

While the pasta is cooking, heat up the olive oil and gently infuse the garlic in the oil for 2 minutes over a medium heat. Drain the pasta and toss in the garlic oil. Season with salt and pepper, then serve immediately.

Vegetable Tempura

A selection of crisp vegetables, such as radish,
   fennel, carrot, broccoli, cauliflower
Large leaf herbs, such as sage
Sunflower oil, for frying
Dipping sauce, to serve

Tempura batter:
2 egg whites
140g plain flour, sifted
A pinch of salt
Ice-cold sparkling water

Prepare the vegetables by washing, peeling if necessary and drying them. Cut them into bite-sized pieces. Wash the herb leaves.

Whisk the egg whites in a bowl with a fork until frothy, then add the flour, salt and sparkling water, which must be really cold. You will need enough water to make the batter up to 250ml. Mix together with the fork – work lightly to avoid making a lumpy batter.

Heat the oil in a deep pan – you need enough to cover the vegetables when they are dropped in the pan. Test the oil by dripping in a little of the batter and see if it crisps up; if it does, the oil is hot enough.

Dip a vegetable into the batter and quickly lower it into the hot oil. Count to about 10 and it should be cooked and golden. Using a slotted spoon, lift out and drain on a plate lined with kitchen paper. Keep warm. Repeat until all the veg are cooked. You can cook 2–3 pieces of veg or herbs at a time, but don't overcrowd the pan as this would lower the temperature of the oil and the batter would go flabby instead of being light and crisp.

Serve with a dipping sauce, such as sweet chilli or a soy-based one, and a cold beer.

Tomato Tart

2–3 good-quality tomatoes
Olive oil
1 tsp balsamic vinegar
Pinch of sugar
¼ tsp prepared garlic
Salt and freshly ground black pepper
1 packet of good-quality store-bought puff pastry (you will only need half,
    but the remainder can be frozen)
1 small egg yolk, beaten
5–6 pitted Kalamata olives

Preheat the oven to 200°C/400°F/gas mark 6.

Cut the tomatoes into chunks and put into a bowl. Pour ½ tablespoon of olive oil,
the balsamic vinegar, sugar, garlic, salt and pepper into a bowl and whisk well.
Pour this over the tomatoes. Heat up a little more olive oil in a frying pan and
gently cook the tomatoes for 3–5 minutes. Set aside.

Roll out the puff pastry so it is approximately 5mm thick and cut it into an 8cm
circle. Fold over 2cm of the pastry to form a border, pressing down firmly.
Transfer the pastry to a baking tray lined with Bake-O-Glide and brush the edges
with beaten egg yolk.

Spoon the cooked tomatoes into the pastry and top with the olives. Bake in the
oven for about 15 minutes. Cool on a wire rack and serve at room temperature
with a rocket and Parmesan salad.

Lemon Spaghetti

80g spaghetti
Zest and juice of 1 large unwaxed lemon
4 tbsp olive oil
2 tbsp freshly grated Parmesan cheese, plus more for serving
5–6 fresh basil leaves
Salt and freshly ground black pepper

Bring a pan of water to a rapid boil and add a good amount of salt to the water. Cook the pasta according to the packet instructions and drain.

Whisk the lemon juice and the zest with the olive oil. Stir in the Parmesan. Season with salt and pepper and taste to adjust – if it needs more lemon juice, olive oil or cheese, then add some.

When the pasta is ready, pour over the lemon sauce and fold in the basil leaves. Serve immediately with more Parmesan.

Truffle Potatoes with Garlic and Cream

1 tsp butter, plus extra for greasing
1 clove of garlic, peeled and cut in half
225ml double cream
½ bottled black truffle, very thinly sliced
Salt and freshly ground black pepper
175g potatoes, peeled and very thinly sliced

Preheat the oven to 180°C/350°F/gas mark 4.

Grease a small ovenproof dish with some butter, then rub the cut side of the garlic all over the dish. Drop the garlic into the double cream with a teaspoon of truffle juice from the bottle and set aside.

Lay two slices of truffle on the bottom of the dish and season with salt and pepper. Put a layer of the potato slices on top of the truffles, then a layer of truffle slices and repeat if there is enough. Season with salt and pepper in between the layers. Remove the garlic from the cream, then pour the cream over the potatoes and season with a little more salt and pepper. Cut the butter up and scatter it over the potatoes.

Cover with foil and bake in the oven for 15 minutes. Remove the foil and continue baking for a further 15–20 minutes or until golden. Serve with a crisp green salad made from curly endive.

Tomato, Mozzarella and Garlic-stuffed Red Pepper

1 large red pepper
1 tomato
1 anchovy fillet in olive oil, chopped, optional
¼ tsp prepared garlic or 2 thin slices of garlic
2 stalks of fresh oregano
Freshly ground black pepper
1 tbsp good-quality olive oil
100g mozzarella cheese, thickly sliced
Crusty bread, to serve

Preheat the oven to 180°C/350°F/gas mark 4.

Cut the pepper in half, leaving the stalk intact if possible, and remove all the seeds. Place the pepper halves on a shallow baking tray. Cut the tomato in half and place a piece in each pepper half. Scatter over the chopped anchovy, if using, and garlic slices, distributing them evenly.

Pull the oregano leaves from the stalks and tuck them into the pepper halves as well. Season with pepper, then lay the mozzarella over the tomatoes and spoon over the olive oil.

Bake in the oven for 20–25 minutes. Serve with any juices and lots of crusty bread.

MORE TIME

Vegetarian

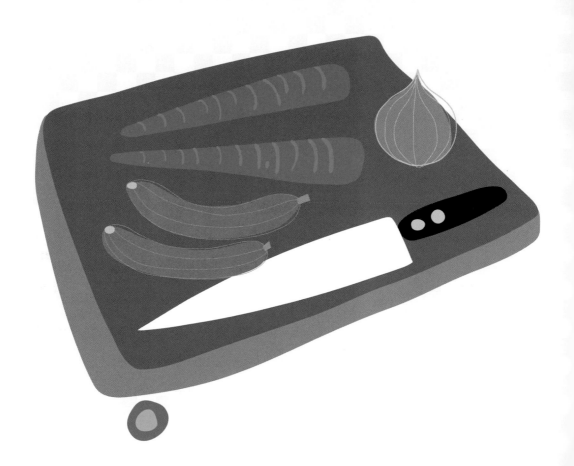

Potato, Leek and Cheese Tart

15g unsalted butter, cubed, plus extra for greasing the dish
1 large waxy potato, peeled
1 leek, cleaned, trimmed and thinly sliced
Salt and freshly ground black pepper
50g Munster cheese, sliced
2–3 tbsp double cream
1 packet of good store-bought puff pastry – you will only need
    a quarter of it, but the remainder can be frozen (or use the
    savoury pastry recipe on page 000)
1 egg yolk

Preheat the oven to 190°C/375°F/gas mark 5. Grease a round ovenproof dish with some of the butter.

Cook the whole potato in a saucepan of boiling water until it is just tender, but not cooked through. Remove with a slotted spoon, drain and slice. Cook the leek slices in the same water for 1–2 minutes until soft. Drain well.

Put the potato slices at the bottom of the dish, spread the leeks on top and season with salt and pepper. Place the cheese slices on top and spoon over the cream.

Roll out the pastry and place over the top, tucking the pastry down the sides as you would for a tarte Tatin. Brush the top with a beaten egg yolk. Bake in the oven for 40–45 minutes. When it is golden and puffed up, remove from the oven and invert onto a serving plate. Serve warm with a green salad.

Asparagus Risotto

4 thick asparagus spears
1 tbsp olive oil
1 shallot, peeled and finely chopped
Salt and freshly ground black pepper
A grating of garlic, or ½ tsp ready-prepared garlic
50g risotto rice
¼ glass of white wine
150ml hot chicken stock, plus a little more, if needed
5–6 fresh mint leaves – chop when ready to use
25g Parmesan cheese, grated
Generous knob of butter

To prepare the asparagus, hold each spear between your two hands and bend it – the spear will snap at the natural woody point so there is no guesswork involved when trimming it. Tidy the ends up with a knife if necessary.

Bring a large shallow pan of water up to the boil and cook the asparagus spears for 3–5 minutes or until they are tender – don't overcook them. Drain and cut into bite-sized pieces and set aside.

Heat the olive oil in a heavy-based frying pan over a medium heat. Add the shallot and soften but do not colour. Season with salt and pepper, then add the garlic and risotto rice, stirring all the time to coat the rice in the onion and oil mixture until the rice is translucent. Pour in the wine and stir until it has almost evaporated, then add a ladle of the hot stock, stir and bring to the boil, then turn down the heat and continue adding the stock, stirring constantly, until it is all used up.

When the liquid has nearly all been absorbed and the rice is tender but still with a bit of a bite, take the pan off the heat and stir in the Parmesan and butter. Add the asparagus and mint. Check the seasoning and serve with a green salad.

Asparagus Mousse

Butter, for greasing
100g asparagus
150ml double cream
1 egg yolk and 1 whole egg, beaten together
Salt and freshly ground black pepper
Lemon juice
Olive oil

Preheat the oven to 160°C/325°F/gas mark 3. Line a small roasting tin with a tea towel. Butter 2 ramekins and place them on the tea towel in the roasting tin. Set aside.

To prepare the asparagus, take each spear, hold it between your two hands and bend it – the spear will snap at the natural woody point so there is no guess work involved when trimming it. Bring a pan of water to the boil, add some salt and blanche the asparagus for 2 minutes. Drain and refresh it in iced water, then drain again. Cut off the tips and reserve, and chop the remainder into small pieces.

Pour half the cream into a saucepan, add the chopped asparagus and simmer for a few minutes until the asparagus is really tender. Blend the mixture with a potato masher or fork, then add the remaining cream. Stir into the eggs and season with salt and pepper. Strain the mousse mixture into the ramekins and then pour boiling water into the tin so that it comes halfway up the sides of the ramekins. Carefully slide the tin into the oven and cook for about 20 minutes or until the mousse has set.

Serve the mousse with the asparagus tips tossed in a little lemon juice and with good-quality olive oil and bread.

Cheese and Rice Soufflé

1½ tsp butter, plus extra for greasing
45g rice
20g Parmesan cheese, grated
50g Cheddar cheese, grated
1 tsp plain flour
125ml milk
1 egg yolk
Pinch of cayenne pepper
Pinch of salt
1 egg white, stiffly beaten

Preheat the oven to 200°C/400°F/gas mark 6.

Grease a small soufflé dish and dust with Parmesan. Tip out the excess cheese and mix with the grated Cheddar.

Cook the rice in a pan of boiling water for 8–10 minutes, then drain.

Make a roux by melting the butter in a small saucepan. Add the flour and stir in well, then add the milk slowly, whisking until smooth. Next add the egg yolk and cheese and stir until cheese has melted. Stir in the cayenne pepper, salt and rice and mix well. Remove the pan from the heat. Fold in the egg white very gently, then pour into the soufflé dish.

Place the dish in the middle of the oven and cook for 20–25 minutes until well risen and golden on top. Serve immediately with a green salad.

Baby Pumpkin Gratin

1 baby pumpkin
A knob of butter
Olive oil
1 Portobello mushroom, sliced
1½ tbsp double cream
50g Gruyère cheese, grated
Salt and freshly ground black pepper

Preheat the oven to 190°C/375°F/gas mark 5.

Cut the top off the pumpkin, about one-quarter of the way down, and remove the seeds and fibres. Smear the inside of the pumpkin with the butter. Place on a baking tray.

Heat a little oil in a frying pan and fry the mushroom until soft. Fill the pumpkin with the mushroom, then pour in the cream and cheese. Mix and season with salt and pepper. Place the pumpkin in an ovenproof dish, cover the top with foil and bake for 40–45 minutes or until the flesh of the pumpkin is soft. Serve with a green salad and a hunk of country bread.

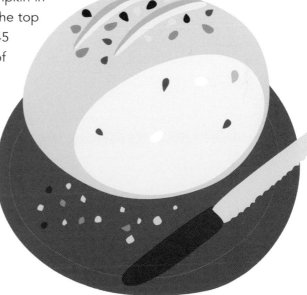

Fennel with New Potatoes and Gorgonzola

6 new potatoes, chopped into chunks
1 small fennel bulb, cut into quarters
1 clove of garlic, peeled
Juice of ½ a lemon
150ml double cream
25g Parmesan cheese, grated
75g Gorgonzola cheese, cubed
Salt
20g unsalted butter, cut into cubes, plus extra for greasing
2 ciabatta crispbreads, crumbled

Preheat the oven to 200°C/400°F/gas mark 6. Butter a small ovenproof dish.

Put the potatoes, fennel and garlic clove into a saucepan of water. Squeeze in the lemon juice, and add some salt to the water. Bring to the boil and cook until the potatoes and fennel are tender. Using a slotted spoon, transfer the potatoes and fennel to the ovenproof dish. Tip away most of the water, reserving 2 tablespoons in the saucepan with the garlic clove.

Add the cream to the cooking water, bring back to the boil and reduce until thick. Mash the garlic with a potato masher and add the Parmesan and Gorgonzola cheeses. Season to taste. Pour the creamy sauce over the potatoes and fennel and top with the butter cubes. Bake for 20–25 minutes or until crispy and golden, then sprinkle over the breadcrumbs and serve.

Home-made Pizza

This dough recipe will make two pizza bases, so any unused dough can be rolled out and frozen, wrapped in clingfilm. For a quick pizza, use a thick slice of toasted focaccia bread as the base.

Pizza dough:
40g fresh yeast
125ml milk, at room temperature
175ml hand-hot water
300g '00' flour, sifted
40g strong plain flour, sifted
3g salt
Olive oil, for greasing the bowl

Pizza toppings:
Good thick tomato sauce
Buffalo mozzarella cheese, thinly sliced
Large basil leaves

Proof the yeast with the milk and water by crumbling the yeast into the liquid and leaving for 10 minutes.

Mix the yeast with the sifted flours and knead for 10 minutes – the dough should be sticky. Add more flour if necessary. Whatever happens, you must not end up with stable dough – it should be threatening to stick to the bowl. Let it rise in an oiled bowl in a warm place for about 1 hour until doubled in size.

Shape half the dough into a pizza shape – pull and stretch it, but do not roll. Let it rise for about 10 minutes. Preheat the oven to 180°C/350°F/gas mark 4.

Spoon on about 2 tablespoons of tomato sauce and spread out over the pizza dough. Scatter over the basil, then cover with mozzarella. Put on to a hot pizza stone or heavy baking sheet and bake for 15 minutes. Eat straight away.

Truffled Scrambled Eggs

If you have never eaten a truffle before, treat yourself and start with this recipe.

Truffled eggs:
1 black truffle, approximately 30g
12 organic eggs, as fresh as possible

Brush the truffle lightly with a soft brush or damp cloth and scrape away any spots of dirt with a sharp knife. You will need a lidded container large enough to hold all the eggs and the truffle. Carefully lay the eggs in the container, put the truffle in the middle of them and close the lid. Store the eggs with the truffle for at least 3 days. You can use more eggs if you wish.

3 truffled eggs (see above)
1 black truffle (see above)
Salt
Splash of double cream
Knob of unsalted butter
Bread, toasted to coincide with the eggs being ready

To make the scrambled eggs, crack the eggs into a glass bowl. Cut the truffle into small dice and add half to the eggs. Add a little salt and cream and beat the eggs gently. Melt some of the butter in a large non-stick pan and pour in the eggs. Stir the eggs constantly with a wooden fork or spoon until they just start to form soft curds. Remove from the heat and add the remaining butter and truffle. Stir until the mixture is cooked but still soft and moist. Butter the toast and spoon the scrambled eggs on top. Serve with a rocket or watercress salad or on its own. Eat straight away and enjoy!

The remaining truffled eggs can be used in other recipes (see page 131).

TREAT YOURSELF

Desserts and Baking

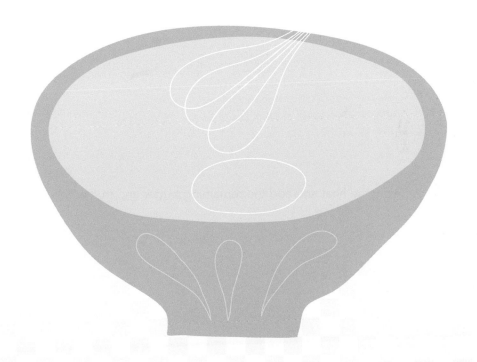

Pastry for One

Savoury:
175g plain flour
115g butter, cold and cubed
1 egg, from the fridge
Salt and freshly ground black pepper
A little cold water, if needed

Sweet:
175g plain flour
115g butter, cold and cubed
1 egg, from the fridge
½ tbsp caster sugar
A little cold water, if needed

Put all the ingredients for either the savoury or sweet pastry into a food processor and pulse until it comes together to form a ball. Only add water if it is crumbly. Wrap in clingfilm and rest in the fridge for at least 30 minutes. Bring to room temperature and roll out.

This will line a 18cm tart tin or make 4 pastry rounds 10cm in diameter. To freeze the pastry, divide into four equal pieces, wrap well in clingfilm or in a small freezer bag, and freeze.

Poached Pears
with Sweet Wine Sauce

Enough sweet pudding wine to cover the pears
1 tbsp golden caster sugar
2 pears, peeled but stalks left on
Double cream, to serve

Put the wine and sugar into a saucepan. Bring up to the boil and stir until all the sugar has dissolved. Place the pears in the boiling liquid, reduce the heat and simmer for 15 minutes or until they are tender. Remove the pan from the heat and leave the pears in the liquid for about 20 minutes, turning them from time to time.

Using a slotted spoon, transfer the pears to a bowl. Bring the poaching liquor to the boil, then simmer to reduce until syrupy. Pour the syrup over the pears and set aside to cool. Serve with thick double cream.

Hot Chocolate Sauce

50g butter
50g good-quality dark chocolate, broken into pieces
125g soft brown sugar
2 tbsp cocoa powder
200g evaporated milk
1 tsp vanilla bean paste or extract

Melt the chocolate and butter together in small pan over a gentle heat. Beat in the sugar and cocoa powder until smooth. Slowly pour in the evaporated milk, stirring all the time. Add the vanilla bean paste and stir. Bring to the boil, then turn down the heat and continue to boil gently for 1 minute. Remove from the heat and set aside. To re-heat, gently bring up to a simmer or keep warm over a bowl of hot water. Great poured over vanilla ice cream.

Baked Orange

1 orange
1 tbsp soft butter
1 tbsp granulated sugar
Double cream, to serve

Preheat the oven to 190°C/375°F/gas mark 5.

Peel the orange, split into two halves and place cut-side up in an ovenproof dish. Spread with the butter and spoon over the sugar. Add 2 tablespoons of water to the dish. Bake for 20–25 minutes and serve with thick double cream.

Baked Bananas

Butter, for greasing
1–2 bananas, peeled and sliced lengthways in half
1½ tbsp brown sugar
Some juice and zest of 1 lemon
1 tbsp Malibu liqueur
Double cream, to serve

Preheat the oven to 200°C/400°F/gas mark 6. Butter a shallow ovenproof dish.

Place the banana in the dish and sprinkle over the sugar, a scraping of lemon zest, a squeeze of lemon juice and 1½ tablespoons of water.

Bake in the oven for 6–7 minutes, then pour over the Malibu and continue baking for another 15 minutes or until the banana is brown and the juice is syrupy. Serve with lots of double cream.

Gelato Affogato

2 scoops of vanilla ice cream
1 shot of hot espresso
½ tbsp toasted almond slivers

Put the ice cream into a heatproof glass and pour the espresso over. Top with the toasted almonds and eat immediately.

Tiramisu

2 shots of cold espresso
Splash of Kahlua
3 sponge finger biscuits
1 small egg yolk
100g mascarpone cheese
½ tbsp icing sugar, or to taste
Cocoa, for dusting
Dark chocolate, chopped or shaved, to decorate

Put the espresso and Kahlua into a bowl and add the biscuits. Soak for 1–2 minutes or until they are completely saturated. Put them into a small glass bowl or wide glass tumbler.

Beat the egg yolk with the mascarpone and sugar. Spoon on to the soaked biscuits. Dust with the cocoa powder and top with the chopped or shaved dark chocolate.

Golden Syrup Pudding

Butter, for greasing
2 tbsp golden syrup
½ a slice of thick-sliced good-quality white bread
1 egg
1 tbsp double cream

Preheat the oven to 190°C/375°F/gas mark 5.

Thickly butter the inside of a ramekin and pour the golden syrup on the bottom. Butter the bread and cut it to fit inside the ramekin. Beat the egg with the cream and pour over the bread. Stand for 5–10 minutes, then bake for 10–15 minutes or until it has puffed up and is golden. Serve with ice cream or clotted cream.

Rice Pudding

½ tbsp butter
1 heaped tbsp pudding rice
½ tbsp sugar
150ml milk
1 tbsp double cream

Preheat the oven to 200°C/400°F/gas mark 6.

Melt the butter in an ovenproof saucepan. Tip in the rice and stir so that every grain is coated. Add the sugar and stir. Pour in the milk and cream, bring to the boil, stir and transfer to the oven for 15 minutes.

After 15 minutes, check the rice pudding – if it looks dry, add a little extra milk. Cook for a further 15–20 minutes or until the rice is tender.

Roasted Fruit with Caramel Sauce

This caramel sauce will keep in the fridge for up to 3 weeks. It is not worth making a smaller amount of this as it keeps so well.

1–2 ripe fruits such as plums, nectarines, peaches, apricots,
   cut in half and stone removed
1–2 tbsp dark brown sugar
A knob of butter
Vanilla ice cream, to serve

Caramel sauce:
50g butter
150g golden syrup
75g soft brown sugar
50g unrefined granulated sugar
100ml double cream
¼ tsp vanilla bean paste or vanilla extract

To make the sauce, melt the butter, golden syrup and both sugars together in a pan over a low heat until the sugar has dissolved. Let it bubble gently for a few minutes but do not let it burn. Slowly pour in the double cream, stirring all the time. Stir in the vanilla bean paste. Bring to the boil, remove from the heat and stir. Set aside.

Preheat the grill to its highest setting. Put the fruit in a heatproof dish, spoon over the sugar and place a little piece of butter in the hollow. Put the fruit under the grill, about 10cm from the heat, and cook for 8–10 minutes until golden brown. Serve with the caramel sauce and vanilla ice cream.

Scones

This recipe makes about 6–8 scones, but they are ideal for freezing.

225g self-raising flour
1½ tbsp caster sugar
Pinch of salt
40g butter, softened and cut into pieces
150ml milk
Beaten egg, to glaze

Preheat the oven to 190°C/375°F/gas mark 5. Line a baking tray with Bake-O-Glide.

Combine the flour, sugar and salt in the bowl of an electric mixer with the paddle hook. Add the butter in pieces, then add the milk to the flour and butter. Mix until the dough just starts to hold together. Turn out on to a floured surface. Roll the dough 2cm thick and cut out with a fluted cutter. Place on the baking tray and brush with beaten egg. Sprinkle over a little more sugar if you wish.

Slide the baking tray into the oven and bake for 8–10 minutes or until the scones are golden. Remove from the oven and cool on a wire rack. To freeze, wrap in clingfilm or a small freezer bag.

Rhubarb Crumble

This makes two servings of crumble topping. Keep the remainder in the fridge until required.

> 1 stick of rhubarb, cut into small pieces
> 1 piece of stem ginger, finely chopped
>
> *Crumble:*
> 25g plain flour
> 25g very cold unsalted butter
> 25g golden granulated sugar
> Brown sugar, for the final topping

Preheat the oven to 180°C/350°F/gas mark 4.

Poach the rhubarb in a pan of water for 1 minute. Drain and spoon into a ramekin and add the chopped stem ginger.

To make the crumble, sift the flour into a bowl and rub in the butter. When the mixture resembles coarse breadcrumbs, mix in the sugar. Spoon the crumble topping over the rhubarb and sprinkle over some more brown sugar. Put the dish on a shallow baking tray and cook for 10–12 minutes or until the fruit is tender and the topping is cooked.

Baked Apple with Custard

1 Bramley apple, cored and scored horizontally
A few blackberries
1 tbsp golden caster sugar
A knob of butter
Demerara sugar, for serving

Custard:
2 large egg yolks
1 tsp cornflour
300ml milk
1 whole vanilla pod, split
1½ tbsp caster sugar

Preheat the oven to 190°C/375°F/gas mark 5.

Put the blackberries into the hole left by the core of the apple to come three-quarters of the way up the apple. Spoon over the sugar and butter. Put the apple into a shallow baking tray and bake for 20–25 minutes or until it is done – this will depend on the size of the apple.

To make the custard, whisk together the egg yolks and cornflour in a bowl, then set aside. Pour the milk into a pan, scrape the vanilla pod seeds into the milk and add the sugar. Gently bring to a simmer. Take the milk off the heat and add to the egg yolk little by little, whisking constantly until it is all combined. Tip the mixture back into the pan and stir over a gentle heat until it coats the back of a wooden spoon. Serve hot or cold.

Serve the baked apple with more demerara sugar and the custard.

TREAT YOURSELF
Drinks

Sugar Syrup

If you enjoy making cocktails, then it is a good idea to have a bottle of sugar syrup in the fridge. It keeps for a few months. Use a mug of any size for measuring.

4 mugfuls of granulated sugar
2 mugfuls of hot water

Put the sugar and water into a saucepan and gently heat to dissolve the sugar. Cool the syrup, then decant into an empty sterilised bottle and seal.

Tom Collins

To mix this cocktail you will need a cocktail shaker, crushed ice and sugar syrup.

50ml gin
25ml fresh lemon juice
25ml sugar syrup (see above)
Soda water
Crushed ice
Thin slice of lemon, for garnish

Fill the cocktail shaker with ice, add the gin, lemon juice and sugar syrup. Shake well, then strain into an ice-filled glass. Top up with soda, stir and decorate with the lemon slice.

Mint Julep

   10 fresh mint leaves, plus extra to garnish
   25ml sugar syrup (see page 167)
   25ml bourbon
   Dash of Angostura Bitters
   Icing sugar, for garnish

Combine the mint and sugar syrup in a cocktail shaker. Gently bruise the mint with a spoon. Fill with crushed ice and pour over the bourbon and a dash of bitters. Shake well and strain into a silver tumbler or glass filled with crushed ice. Garnish with mint leaves with icing sugar sifted over them.

Hendrick's Gin and Cucumber

   2 measures Hendrick's Gin
   3cm piece of cucumber, seeded and cut into matchsticks
   Tonic water, to taste
   Ice

Mix all the ingredients together in a tall, clear glass.

Jongy's Cocktail

This is an after-dinner cocktail, with two versions.

Jongy 1:
25ml vodka
25ml Kahlua
1 shot of cold espresso
½ vanilla pod or a drop of vanilla extract
Ice

Pour all the ingredients into a highball glass with lots of ice and stir well using the vanilla pod.

Jongy 2:
25ml vodka
25ml Kahlua
1 shot of hot espresso
½ vanilla pod or a drop of vanilla extract
Double cream

Put the vodka, Kahlua, espresso and vanilla into a wine glass. Float the double cream on top of the alcohol by pouring it slowly over the back of the spoon.

Campari Cocktail

50ml Campari
50ml sweet vermouth
Ice
Soda water
Fresh orange slice, to garnish

Pour the Campari and vermouth into a tall glass
filled with ice. Top up with soda water and stir gently.
Decorate with a slice of fresh orange.

Cosmopolitan

25ml orange-flavoured vodka
25ml Cointreau
15ml lime cordial
75ml cranberry juice
1 piece of orange peel
Ice

Shake all the ingredients with ice
in a cocktail shaker and strain into
a chilled martini glass.

Elderflower Cordial

1.5 litres still mineral water
20 perfect elderflower heads
Zest and juice of 4 organic lemons
85g citric acid (available from the chemist)
1.8kg golden caster sugar

Boil the water in a stainless steel pan, remove from the heat and stir in the sugar. Cover with a clean tea towel and leave to cool.

When the water has cooled, stir in the elderflower heads, lemon zest and juice, citric acid and sugar. Cover with a clean tea towel and leave for 4–5 days in a cool, dark area. Strain into sterilised bottles and seal. Leave for 1 month before using.

Dilute to taste with sparkling or still mineral water and serve with ice. I also like to pour some cordial over strawberries and raspberries before serving.

Old-fashioned Lemonade

10 organic lemons
2.5 litres water
335g unrefined caster sugar (or more to taste)
Ice, to serve

Peel the lemons using a potato peeler, leaving behind as much of the white pith as possible. Put the peel into a large pan and add the water. Bring to the boil.

Put the juice of the lemons and the sugar into a large heatproof container and stir to combine. Pour the boiling water on to the lemon juice and sugar and stir until dissolved. Cool and serve chilled with lots of ice.

Index

alpine eggs 19
apples: autumn apples and
  bacon 37
  baked apple with custard
  165
  Worcestershire toast 25
apricots: chicken and apricot
  salad 48
  chicken with prunes and 52
Arbroath smokie with Pernod
  and crème fraîche 90
artichoke hearts on toast 27
Asian seared beef salad 70
asparagus: asparagus and
  lemon pasta 130
  asparagus mousse 149
  asparagus risotto 148
  gulls' eggs with 124
avocado, bacon, lettuce and
  tomato sandwich 28–9

bacon: autumn apples and
  bacon 37
  bacon, lettuce, avocado and
  tomato sandwich 28–9
  baked potato topping 30
  calves' liver and bacon 41
  devils on horseback 20
bananas, baked 159
beef: Asian seared beef salad
  70
  baked onion stuffed with
  minced meat 64
  beef Stroganoff 65
  blue cheese burger 38–9
  Bolognese sauce 62–3
  steak in Bloody Mary
  marinade 66
  steak sandwich 61
  steak with savoury butter
  36–7
Bircher muesli 12
black cab kippers 101
blackberries, pan-fried pigeon
  breast with cassis and 54
blinis, potato 120
Bolognese sauce 62–3
bourbon: mint julep 168
bread: croque monsieur 18
  French toast with fried
  tomatoes 17

refrigerator bread 14
  toast 23
  tomato and bread soup 22
broad beans: spaghetti with
  pecorino and 137
  with prosciutto and ricotta
  cheese 56
broccoli: chicken and broccoli
  bake 47
bubble and squeak 55
burger, blue cheese 38–9

cabbage: bubble and squeak
  55
Campari cocktail 170
caramel sauce, roasted fruit
  with 162
Cheddar pudding 127
cheese: alpine eggs 19
  autumn apples and bacon 37
  baby pumpkin gratin 151
  blue cheese burger 38–9
  broad beans with prosciutto
  and ricotta cheese 56
  Cheddar pudding 127
  cheese and rice soufflé 150
  chicken and Roquefort salad
  45
  croque monsieur 18
  endive salad with Manchego
  cheese and fried quails'
  eggs 134
  fennel with new potatoes and
  Gorgonzola 152
  goats' cheese soufflé
  pudding 133
  Gorgonzola and mascarpone
  pasta bake 126
  grilled figs wrapped in Parma
  ham with Gorgonzola 21
  honeyed pears with
  Gorgonzola and thyme 123
  mac and cheese 57
  penne pasta with taleggio
  cheese 139
  Portobello mushrooms with
  melted Brie 138
  potato, leek and cheese tart
  147
  potted ham and cheese 24
  tomato, mozzarella and
  garlic-stuffed red pepper
  145
  Welsh rarebit 30, 61

Worcestershire toast 25
chestnuts, pheasant with thyme
  and 53
chick-peas: hummus 114–15
chicken: chicken and apricot
  salad 48
  chicken and broccoli bake 47
  chicken and lobster salad
  78–9
  chicken and Roquefort salad
  45
  chicken Milanese with fennel
  slaw 46–7
  chicken salad with honey and
  almond dressing 49
  chicken thighs with coconut
  and almonds 76
  devilled chicken 50
  Thai green curry 75
  with apricots and prunes 52
  with creamy mustard sauce 44
  with honey and orange 51
chicken livers pan-fried with
  tomatoes 43
chocolate: hot chocolate sauce
  158
  potted chicken 74
cod: fish and chips 112
coffee: gelato affogato 160
  tiramisu 160
Cosmopolitan 171
crab: chilled tomato soup with
  cucumber and 32
  crab and chilli linguini 103
  crab crostini 98
  crab spring rolls with lemon
  oil 118–19
  potted crab with sourdough
  toast 121
  Thai-style fish cakes 108
croque monsieur 18
crostini, crab 98
crumble, rhubarb 164
curries: cold curried prawns 111
  Thai green curry 75
custard 165

devils on horseback 20
Dover sole with lemon butter
  94–5
duck: duck in green
  peppercorn sauce 84
  with apples, cranberries and
  oranges 81

eggs: alpine eggs 19
  baked egg with spinach 128
  baked eggs with black truffle 131
  eggs Florentine 132
  endive salad with Manchego cheese and fried quails' eggs 134
  gulls' eggs with asparagus spears 124
  truffled scrambled eggs 154
elderflower cordial 172
endive salad with Manchego cheese and fried quails' eggs 134

fennel: chicken Milanese with fennel slaw 46–7
  fennel and lentil soup 33
  with new potatoes and Gorgonzola 152
figs wrapped in Parma ham with Gorgonzola 21
fish and chips 112
fish cakes, Thai-style 108
French toast with fried tomatoes 17
fruit: roasted fruit with caramel sauce 162
  smoothies 13

gelato affogato 160
gin cocktails 167, 168
goats' cheese soufflé pudding 133
golden syrup pudding 161
Gorgonzola and mascarpone pasta bake 126
grouse with orange and juniper 82–3
gulls' eggs with asparagus spears 124

ham: croque monsieur 18
  grilled figs wrapped in Parma ham with Gorgonzola 21
  potted ham and cheese 24
hash browns with fried onions and mushrooms 125
Hendrick's gin and cucumber 168
hummus 114–15

ice cream: gelato affogato 160
Italian sausages with grilled pepper and onion 77

Jongy's cocktail 169

kedgeree 107
kippers: black cab kippers 101
  potted kippers on toast 20

lamb: chop with savoury butter 36–7
  cutlets in puff pastry 68
  loin with Parmesan and basil crust 42
  rack with basil cream 73
  slow-cooked lamb 60
langoustines with garlic butter sauce 89
leeks: leeks vinaigrette with potted shrimps 104
  potato, leek and cheese tart 147
lemon spaghetti 143
lemonade, old-fashioned 173
lentils: fennel and lentil soup 33
liver: calves' liver and bacon 41
  pan-fried chicken livers with tomatoes 43
lobster: chicken and lobster salad 78–9
  grilled lobster with ginger sauce 110
  lobster cocktail 117

mac and cheese 57
mackerel with hummus and pitta bread 114–15
mayonnaise 78
melon: sweet, hot and sour melon with prosciutto 16
mint julep 168
moules marinières 87
mousse, asparagus 149
muesli, Bircher 12
muffins, good morning 11
mushrooms: baked potato topping 30
  beef Stroganoff 65
  hash browns with fried onions and 125
  Portobello mushrooms with melted Brie 138

mussels: moules marinières 87
  Normandy mussels 116

Normandy mussels 116

oats: Bircher muesli 12
  porridge 13
olives: baked potato topping 31
onions: baked onion stuffed with minced meat 64
  fried onion rings 28–9
oranges: baked orange 158
  pork chop with 67
oysters with champagne sauce 109

pasta: asparagus and lemon pasta 130
  crab and chilli linguini 103
  Gorgonzola and mascarpone pasta bake 126
  lemon spaghetti 143
  mac and cheese 57
  penne pasta with taleggio cheese 139
  spaghetti pangrattato 136
  spaghetti with garlic and olive oil 140
  spaghettini with prawns, garlic and cherry tomatoes 93
  with fresh tomato and basil sauce 135
pastry for one 156
pears: honeyed pears with Gorgonzola and thyme 123
  poached pears with sweet wine sauce 157
penne pasta with taleggio cheese 139
peppers: Italian sausages with grilled pepper and onion 77
  tomato, mozzarella and garlic-stuffed red pepper 145
pheasant: devilled pheasant 50
  with chestnuts and thyme 53
  with walnuts and Madeira 85
pigeon breast with blackberries and cassis 54
pine nut and raisin pilaf 129
pizza, home-made 153
pork: chop with oranges 67
  chop with savoury butter 36–7

spare ribs with ginger, chillies and garlic 71
spring pork stir-fry 35
porridge 13
Portobello mushrooms with melted Brie 138
potatoes: baked potatoes 29–31
bubble and squeak 55
fennel with new potatoes and Gorgonzola 152
fish and chips 112
hash browns with fried onions and mushrooms 125
potato blinis with smoked salmon and sour cream 120
potato, leek and cheese tart 147
smoked salmon rosti 105
truffle potatoes with garlic and cream 144
prawns: cold curried prawns 111
grilled tiger prawns 100
salt and pepper prawns 97
spaghettini with prawns, garlic and cherry tomatoes 93
Thai-style fish cakes 108
prosciutto, broad beans with ricotta cheese and 56
prunes: chicken with apricots and 52
devils on horseback 20
pumpkin gratin 151

quail with rosemary and quince 80

refrigerator bread 14
rhubarb crumble 164
rice: asparagus risotto 148
cheese and rice soufflé 150
kedgeree 107
pine nut and raisin pilaf 129
rice pudding 161
risotto with black and white truffles 58
rosti, smoked salmon 105

salads: Asian seared beef 70
chicken and apricot 48
chicken and lobster 78–9

chicken and Roquefort 45
chicken with honey and almond dressing 49
endive with Manchego cheese and fried quails' eggs 134
salmon: escalope with cream sauce 91
with a herb crust 98
salt and pepper prawns 97
sandwiches 28–9, 61
sardines with celery and pine nuts 88
sausages with grilled pepper and onion 77
scallops: grilled with fennel and hazelnuts 113
with lemon, black olives and capers 95
scones 163
sea bass with caper and orange butter 102
shrimps: leeks vinaigrette with potted shrimps 104
smoked haddock: Arbroath smokie with Pernod and crème fraîche 91
kedgeree 107
with crème fraîche and chives 96
smoked salmon: potato blinis with sour cream and 120
smoked salmon rosti 105
smoothies 13
sole with lemon butter 94–5
soufflé, cheese and rice 150
soups: chilled tomato with cucumber and crab 32
fennel and lentil 33
tomato and bread 22
sour cream: baked potato topping 31
spaghetti: lemon spaghetti 143
spaghetti pangrattato 136
spaghettini with prawns, garlic and cherry tomatoes 93
with broad beans and pecorino 137
with garlic and olive oil 140
spare ribs with ginger, chillies and garlic 71

spinach: baked egg with 128
eggs Florentine 132
spring rolls, crab 118–19
squid with tartar sauce 92
steak see beef
sugar syrup 167
sweetbreads in a cream sauce 72

tarts: potato, leek and cheese 147
tomato 142
tempura, vegetable 141
Thai green curry 75
Thai-style fish cakes 108
tiramisu 160
toast 23
Tom Collins 167
tomatoes: baked potato toppings 30, 31
chilled tomato soup with cucumber and crab 32
French toast with fried tomatoes 17
pan-fried chicken livers with 43
pasta with fresh tomato and basil sauce 135
steak in Bloody Mary marinade 66
tomato and bread soup 22
tomato, mozzarella and garlic-stuffed red pepper 145
tomato tart 142
trout with hazelnuts 115
truffles: baked eggs with black truffle 131
risotto with black and white truffles 58
truffle potatoes with garlic and cream 144
truffled scrambled eggs 154

veal: escalope with tarragon sauce 40
veal saltimbocca 39
vegetable tempura 141
venison steak with juniper berries 69
vodka cocktails 169, 171

Welsh rarebit 30, 61
Worcestershire toast 25